I'LL DO IT WHEN I FEEL BETTER

Hugh M. Smith

Depressed Anonymous Publications
Louisville Kentucky   40217

Other Books By Depressed Anonymous Publications

Depressed Anonymous

The Depressed Anonymous Workbook

Higher Thoughts for Down Days

TeenCare

Seniorwise

How to Find Hope

Depressed Once-Not Twice

Shining a Light on the Dark Night of the Soul

The Promises of Depressed Anonymous

Dep-Anon Family Group Manual

Believing is Seeing

DEPRESSSED ANONYMOUS PUBLICATIONS
P.O. Box 17414
Louisville, KY 40217

© 1986, 2013 Depressed Anonymous Publications

All rights reserved. No part of this book may be reproduced or utilized in any form or by any means, electronic or mechanical, including photocopying, recording or by an information storage or retrieval system, without express permission from the publisher, Depressed Anonymous Publications and/or the author.

Website http://www.depressedanon.com
Email depanon@netpenny.net

2nd Edition

ISBN 978-1-929438-15-0

TABLE OF CONTENTS

Introduction i
Acknowledgements viii

CHAPTERS
1. I'll do it when I feel better 1
2. Bill W., (co-founder of Alcoholics Anonymous) and Depression 7
3. What is Depressed Anonymous 22
4. The Promises of DA part 1 28
5. The Promises of DA part 2 41
6. Compulsions and Choices: The addictive nature of depression 54
7. Hope 65
8. Trust 73
9. Spirituality and Depression 84
10. Prayer and Meditation 97
Notes 105
Bibliography/ References 110

An important note to the reader of this work.

All references in this work are to be found on pages 104-111.

References are indicated by a closed parenthesis indicating a particular work. For example (3) indicates a reference to the work Depressed Anonymous.

"I'LL DO IT WHEN I FEEL BETTER."

I have written this book because of a pressing concern. My concern is for those who are depressed and who are at a loss as to how to get help for their depression. From my own personal experience I know now that this procrastination is so serious a problem that it can do nothing but dig a deeper hole. As the old saying goes "if you want to get out of the hole, then quit digging."

We have always known that the human person has always had a hunger 1) to belong and 2) for feeling complete. What you will read in the following chapters will provide, promote and develop the relational tools for belonging to a fellowship and at the same time experience the completeness of a mutual aid group such as Depressed Anonymous.

The beauty of mutual help programs is to promote the wonderful reality that "we are not alone." Dr. David Karp in his excellent work, Speaking of Sadness [1] states correctly that we may be at a juncture where we are ready as a culture to see the wisdom in the spiritual idea that our individual well-being is inseparable from that seamless web of connections.

And today with one in four persons in the US living alone, and most disconnected from each other, know that the driving force in our society and most of the western world, is one that promotes competition and individualism. Who we are, being, has been replaced by what we have. About half of the population in the United States is the result of blended families and families broken by divorce and remarriage. Most of us living in Industrialized Western Cultures are the result growing up in smaller family units and so make our support systems smaller. In the past, our families supported each other in emotional, spiritual and economic ways. Most communities had neighbors whom they knew by first name. Because of changing societal mores and values persons today do not have much of a mooring of self to even pretend to have an identity.

Who am I? What do I want? are questions which gets pushed aside and are reflected upon only in one's life's crises. And so it becomes a fact that we clamor for more things to help keep up our frenetic pace, lifestyles and the resultant isolation that comes from not knowing who we are. One's life becomes an absorption with having and being materially productive that prevents the "i" from being dependent upon the "we", or from even in need of a "we." We end up wondering "is this all there is?"

Have you ever said to yourself, "I'll do it when I feel better?" Most of us have at one point or another said the same I am sure. When I was depressed I often commented that I would have to do something about getting myself undepressed, which is when I felt better and as you might suspect, I never did feel better. And the reason? Because I never did anything about my isolation which was coupled with this uneasy feeling that I was going to be sentenced to a life of grief. I also believed that since I wasn't to blame for my depression then wouldn't those depression symptoms just go away by themselves? At least this was my hope. I believed that since I didn't cause my depressive symptoms (or so I thought) that with time these feelings of despair and this fruitless isolation would just fade away. (And yes, in some cases this may be true, that is, the fog will lift and we will be back on the playing field of life. But for most of us we ask how can we continue to live in the isolation of the depression experience?) Later did I realize that what was happening to me didn't just drop out of the blue. I now knew that If was to get better then I would have to take responsibility for my depressive thoughts and feelings. (We will explain this in more detail in Chapter Six when we discuss the compulsions and choices that are a big part of the depression experience). Again, those of us who are part of the Depressed Anonymous fellowship advocate that when we discover we are depressed we need to take responsibility for our own recovery if we want to feel better. This is the reason that Depressed Anonymous, a 12 Step support group was formed. The fellowship is modeled after Alcoholics Anonymous, a 12 step program which utilizes spiritual principles as the basis for one's personal recovery. I have no doubt that the best way to feel better is to get involved in your own recovery process. You no longer have to believe that you will just have to sweat it out. Now, today, there is a program designed just for you and it works. It works if you force yourself to go to meetings, read the literature, listen to the tapes and talk with other members of the fellowship. With the support of fellow members who have been depressed or are depressed, you will find the love and caring from those who understand your pain. How is that you ask? Well, it's because they have been where you have been and now have found the keys to a new beginning for their lives. Something that might have taken years to construct, namely lifestyles with the self destructive thoughts and behaviors can't be torn down in a day. Our advice to you who want to take the bull by the horns – and not wait till you begin to feel better, we urge that you do something today. Now! By reading the following chapters of this book you will find concrete solutions for overcoming your symptoms of depression. The book can serve as a roadmap that can lead you out of the darkness of despair and into the light of hope. We believe that the antidote to depression is a community of persons bound together in a fellowship and united for a common purpose. And this community group call them fellowships, are where we find solutions to the questions which are always at the front of our minds and which we carry like a heavy burden through our day. This fellowship will provide an individual with an identity, a purpose and a mission which is larger than his/her individual self. This accountability to the fellowship and most importantly to ourselves is what gets us out of bed in the morning. And as we gradually get worn down by the daily burdens of living it is precisely these anxious burdens which suck the life from us as we become more deflated and lifeless, both in mind and body, and I might add, in spirit. These feelings of helplessness and hopelessness produce persons who are isolated and desperate. They feel totally isolated and disconnected from life and from their selves. I know the feeling. I was scared and frightened at what was happening to my memory, my concentration and my need for constant sleep!

THAT VITAL SPIRITUAL EXPERIENCE

We now know that one of the primary routes that for many lead one out of the despair, and can eradicate one's addictions and debilitating attachments is that reality we call "spirituality." As Dr. Karp, a Boston University sociologist discovered in his book SPEAKING OF SADNESS (1), he researched 50 people's responses to questions about how depression affected their lives. His interviews led him into a discussion on how a person's Spirituality related to their own struggle with depression. Here is what he has to say about his experiences: At the same time that my conceptual consciousness was being raised about the connection between spirituality and depression, I was leaving many of my interviews awed at the courage and grace with which certain people faced unimaginable pain and loss. I was especially impressed with those who spoke of their depression as a gift from which they had learned valuable lessons. While I could not relate emotionally or intellectually with visions of reincarnation or explanations of depression as central to a God-given life mission, I left many interviews with a sense that spirituality engaged individual were in touch with something important. The issue was not a matter of evaluating the truth of their particular brand of spirituality. What I felt was a measure of envy of those who displayed an acceptance that seemed to me incongruous with accounts of exceptional pain. These people possessed or knew something that I didn't." (1)

And just like those of Dr. Karp's research, discovering the importance of having a spirituality to carry one through the dark night of the soul we find in Chapter Two how Bill W., discovered and experienced personally the power of the "spirit" for his own recovery from alcoholism. He came to believe that having and developing a vibrant spirituality is the one thing that would make it possible for him as well as for thousands of others suffering from alcoholism not only find sobriety but would give suffering individuals the keys that open the door to a new day lighted with hope and serenity. Once provided with a spirituality, a belief in a power greater than themselves they climbed out of the deep hole and learned new ways of living without the need for that attachment to behaviors that would eventually kill them.

As we continue our discussion of depression and the path that we have taken to deal with it you may be able to trace your own "turning points in your life. You will read in the following pages the "ups and downs" of depression and the responses/solutions making it possible for men and women to find a way out of the prison of their depression. As you continue to absorb the messages provided in this work, and read about others who are journeying through the darkness of depression you may say, "Hey, that's me." And if these chapters do speak to you, and you can identify with what you read here, then it would be well for you to examine the Twelve Steps and see if they may fit your own life experiences.

Bill W.., makes the claim that:

Everyone must agree that we A.A's are unbelievably fortunate people; fortunate that we have suffered so much;

fortunate that we can know, understand, and love each other so supremely well. These attributes and virtues are scarcely of the earned variety. Indeed, most of us are well aware that these are rare gifts which have their true origin in our kinship born of a common suffering and a common deliverance by the grace of God.

Thereby we are privileged to communicate with each other to a degree and in a manner not very often surpassed among our Nonalcoholic friends in the world around us. (2)

In another place Bill writes the following to a friend

"I used to be ashamed of my condition and so didn't talk about it. But nowadays I freely confess I am a depressive, and this has attracted other depressives to me. Working with them has helped a great deal." (2)

Today, the stigma for someone depressed still stalks the minds of many people. People think that since they themselves are depressed (those suffering from depression) it is their fault because they have been told by those who have never been depressed that all they have to do is to pray, do something fun and/or just "snap out of it."

Because they don't see a cast or some other outward sign of sickness in their depressed friend/loved one they might say that the person depressed should just "quit feeling sorry for themselves." In Depressed Anonymous we believe that if a person's depression isn't treated it could spiral down into a life threatening situation. As a 12 Step fellowship we are committed to getting help and so gain empowerment by taking responsibility for ourselves and use whatever means we can, be that medications, therapy and mutual help groups such as Depressed Anonymous. In Chapter Nine, the chapter dealing with Spirituality and Depression, we find a rich assortment of beliefs about the need, the power and the daily support that comes from developing that vital spirituality that begins the process of sustained recovery – one day at a time.

The god that we know speaks to us through members of the Depressed Anonymous group. The Higher Power will put a new sense of purpose into your life once you know how to turn to it and surrender your pain. The Depressed Anonymous group will lead you safely and gently. The miracle is in the group. (3)

Dr. Karp makes the point in the following quote that The estimated 11 to 15 million people suffering from depression and the millions with anxiety disorders are the victims of a society that has lost sight of what I now see as a shared sociological and spirituality. It is that our individual emotional health and the health of society are inseparable if we do not nourish society by realizing our individual responsibilities to it; we pay the price in terms of individual illness. In this way, those millions pained by affective disorders are part of a dialectical process in which the extent of collective suffering eventually creates an urge to change the social structures that have made so many of us ill. During the current moment of cultural discontent we may be better able to appreciate the spiritual message that all of us are connected and responsible to each other. Although we can never return to the small intimate communities of the nineteenth century, such a communitarian vision is the necessary starting place for efforts at social reconnection and thereby the creation of a more generally happy society." (1)

We believe that the start of changing any culture is to begin by initiating the needed change in oneself. I hope that as you read and reflect upon the thoughts presented here in "I'll do it when I feel better" that you will be provided with a new hope and strong desire to discover what the rest of us have already discovered, namely, that there is a way out of the prison of depression. And what you will learn first is that you have the key in your hand.

Gratefully,
Dr. Hugh S.
September 14, 2009

CHAPTER ONE

I'll Do It When I Feel Better

THE DEPRESSED ANONYMOUS STORY
How it all began!

   This is the story of how my own journey down into the valley of tears began. As I remember it began quite suddenly and the experience was similar to feeling myself slide down a hill. And it was at that point that my life changed forever. Unknowingly, my life had taken on a new direction and purpose.

   Gradually, I found it difficult to get out of bed in the morning. I also began to experience a feeling of hollowness gnawing at me from the inside – much like an out of control cancer. This black mood was eating away all that once interested me. I began to feel helpless and out of control. I also felt that I wasn't able to retain mastery over my own direction in life. I began to notice that something was very wrong with the way I was feeling.

   To this day I can tell you exactly the place and time when I began to feel this terrible sadness suddenly and dramatically come upon me. I felt myself sliding down and over a dark precipice from which I was not able to climb out of for over a year of painful months. An unfamiliar feeling of inner pain and numbness descended upon me.

   At the time I truly thought that this descent into hell came from "out of the blue." But like all feelings that we experience, I now know that because of situations in my most recent past, and my reactions to them, that these thoughts and feelings had accumulated a wealth of debt whose note had come due on this particularly warm day in August. Starting with this day, I began to move through a fog that not even will power could lift.

I realized in time that unless I started to do something about the way I felt and take responsibility for myself and my behavior, my situation most probably would worsen.

My own depression with its concomitant restlessness and despair had been developing over a period of a few months as one loss after another began to pile up in my personal life. I also was struggling inwardly with having to move back in with my parents at middle age and having to depend on them for help. At the time I moved back home my Dad was recuperating from a massive heart attack and his health was failing fast. This too was a great personal loss to me. At the same time, I entered a University located in my home town and struggled to earn a Master's degree in Counseling Psychology. The studies did not come easy. Besides this, I also found a job – an entry level position working with minority persons who were unemployed and many of them were depressed. Because of infighting within the administration structure I found this position to be quite burdensome. I looked forward to moving on. With my newly earned Master's degree in hand I entered private practice.

It was at this time that I began to feel like I was walking in a fog. My mind was blank and my feelings were on edge. I felt as if a large hole with jagged edges was located in the center of my psyche. The anxiety was exacerbated by the fact that I was having trouble getting out of bed of a morning. The pain that this hole produced became a daily reminder that something was not right and so I took comfort in sleep. I went to bed as soon as I got off of work. I thought I could shake off with sleep whatever had me by the throat. All that had held an interest for me – all my interests in people – my future career as a therapist – I lost interest in everything. Nothing provided any pleasure for me at this time. My life was on hold. The only thing that I was interested in was sleep. I just wanted to sleep.

During this time my parents, as usual, were most gracious, understanding and supportive following the loss of a career which was due to my substance addiction. They provided me with an unconditional love which provided me with a stable and secure base from which I could try to start my life over again. And so here I was, 45 years old, starting over again with Mom and Dad and feeling much like the child again. The fact that I quit smoking, a few months after my Dad had died, was a contributing factor in my depression. Over the years cigarettes had been a great friend for me. This friend was there when I was happy, when I was nervous, when I had just finished a meal or had a cup of coffee. It was there when I did not know what to do with my hands. It was quite a nice crutch. Much like an alcoholic beverage or that first dip of ice cream.

All of what I have written down so far has to do with creating meaning. Humans have as their occupation to constantly create meaning for their lives. Whatever we do has to have meaning. Most important of all, I felt that I had lost myself. I felt that I too was gone. I had lost touch with my true self. I lost touch with my real self. I felt alone, worthless, and especially unacceptable to myself. During this time I had the thought that if someone were seen laughing or having a good time – this made me angry. How dare anyone could smile while I felt so miserable? This unfamiliar feeling made me think that my brain was made out of cotton. I couldn't shove another thought into my head. It was as if the cells of my brain were filled to the brim. Like they were saying "sorry, we're full."

There was nothing that I could do to shake these horrible and painful feelings. My mind was unable to focus or concentrate on anything. My memory was seriously impaired, it was as a sign was hanging on my forehead declaring "temporarily out of order". I no longer could keep my mind on anything. I found that to read even a paragraph from a book wore me out.

I knew that I had to do something because I was physically and emotionally drained. I was scared. I felt that each new day found my strength gradually ebbing away. I knew that something was wrong – but what was it?

Because of all the losses that I had accumulated over the past few months I began to slip down into that dark abyss known mainly to those who have experienced depression. I had to do something and more than talking to break out of depression – I had to change the way that I lived my life. Somehow I had taken the way I thought, and felt for granted. I didn't realize that feelings over time, especially intense emotions such as fear and pain can cause quite a change in the body. These unpleasant emotions became responsible for a bunch of symptoms that I later knew to be depression. I had to admit that my life was out of control, that I was powerless to overcome my symptoms of depression by will power alone. I needed to believe again in a power bigger than myself. I had to have this "vital spiritual experience" that I heard over and over again in Alcoholic Anonymous meetings. Having been in ministry for many years I thought that I had already had a "vital spiritual experience." So what happened? Could I have lost it along the way? So here's what I did. I began walking five miles a day in a local mall near my home. And this walking took place before I went to my work. I set myself a goal to force myself to walk everyday till I started feeling better. Now, almost a year had gone by since that day in August when I felt myself slipping into the abyss. Then I discovered after doing this exercise for a week or so I started to feel better.

But then the old message came back and told me that "Yes, but this good feeling won't last." The negative voice was right – it didn't last. I continued to walk. And my fear grew so that I thought that I would never feel better again.

I knew if could have had one good day or a lifetime of good days before my depression then I knew that it made sense that I could have a good day again. I kept on walking. In time, and later and with more walking I gradually walked out of and through the fog that had me imprisoned. But I had to do the work! Did my symptoms have me imprisoned or did the meaning that I had created in my mind about my life have me imprisoned? I began to think that it was the meaning that I had given to all those losses that had recently piled up in my life and which gradually threw me to the ground, hog tied me and wouldn't let me go. I had to believe that somehow my walking could lead me out of the prison of depression. I was right as this activity did just that. I no longer felt depressed. And I learned a great lesson here in that "motivation follows action." This has done more for me than anything. It was making myself, forcing myself do something every day to help myself. This in itself turned out to be the motivator that eventually got me out of the abyss. I discovered that by having the belief that "motivation follows action" could help change the way I felt that this would work for others persons who felt immobilized by their depression. As they say in another recovery group, "move the body and the mind will follow." Finally, as we all know, this is the one thing that persons depressed do not want to do--to get moving!

And now let me backtrack a bit here and go to a very important event that was the onal "turning point" for where I am today. Previous to my own depression I had worked one on one with a client named Jane. Now Jane was depressed and confined to her home following quadruple by-pass surgery weeks before. I was learning hands-on counseling and my clinical supervisor asked me to go to her home and see what I could do to help her out. After spending ten weeks counseling Jane, with one session per week, I saw that she started to have more vitality and was acting more spontaneous. She began to regain interest in those things that had given her pleasure before her heart attack. It was these visits with Jane that got me to thinking that if Jane could join together and get into a 12 step group she might get better. She might find the same help that other addicts had found who committed themselves to a program of recovery utilizing the suggested principles of the 12 steps. Just months prior to this situation, in May of 1985, I had started a group now known as Depressed Anonymous. I had the conviction that a person depressed could find the same strength and serenity as did those who, sick and tired of being sick and tired, stumbled into their first Alcoholics Anonymous meeting. So what began as a pilot project at the University, namely gathering depressed people together in a group to talk about their experiences, I discovered that people of all ages and beliefs could gradually get out of the prison of depression. A group, especially if the group followed the suggested 12 steps of the spiritual program known now as Depressed Anonymous, over time, could break the bonds of their depression. So, I discovered how a pilot program that specifically centered around the subject of depression, and set up under the auspices of the University and the local County Mental Health Center could help people escape their isolation and feeling hopeless and helpless. They were no longer alone. It turned out that all the participants of the group got better after a number of months of treatment. Depressed Anonymous was then opened up to the public. What was thought impossible, namely just to get a depressed person motivated, out of bed and to a meeting, turned out to be very possible? To this day Depressed Anonymous continues to spread its influence globally. For that we are grateful.

CHAPTER TWO

BILL W., AND DEPRESSION

In this chapter I will introduce you the thoughts of Bill W., the co-founder of Alcoholics Anonymous. In AS BILL SEES IT, Bill W., makes a number of references to his own experience of depression. I hope that you, the reader will find the thoughts that follow a source of hope and strength for your own life.

I used to be ashamed of my condition and so I didn't talk about it. But nowadays I freely confess I am a depressive, and this has attracted other depressives to me. Working with them has helped a great deal. (2)

Bill W., wrote these words to a friend in a letter and the letter is dated 1954. A note at the bottom of the page said that he has had no depression since 1955.

I am heartened by the fact that Bill Wilson confessed his troubles with depression and how he came to terms with it by speaking out about it. I think that our program of recovery, even though initially based upon Alcoholism, it has been found to help those persons like ourselves who are depressed. In fact the program has a strong spiritual base from which we can find immense support and hope.

Bill states that in my own case, the foundation stone of freedom from fear is that of faith: a faith that despite all worldly appearances to the contrary, causes me to believe that I live in a universe that makes sense.

When I was driven to my knees by alcohol (depression), I was made ready to ask for the gift of faith. And all was changed. Never again, my pains and problems notwithstanding would experience my former desolation. I saw the universe to be lighted by God's love: I was alone no more. (2)

One of the main paths that leads out of the prison of depression is for those of us who are depressed believe that a power greater than ourselves is what is going to set us free. Bill W.., reminds us in the following passage the reality of a power greater than ourselves.

I had always believed in a power greater than myself. I had often pondered these things. I was not an atheist. Few people really are, for that means blind faith in the strange proposition that this universe originated in a cipher and aimlessly rushes nowhere. My intellectual heroes, the chemists, the astronomers, even the evolutionists, suggested vast laws and forces at work. Despite contrary indications, I had little doubt that a mighty purpose and rhythm underlay all. How could there be so much of precise and immutable law, and no intelligence? I simply had to believe in a Spirit of the Universe, who neither knew time nor limitation. But that was as far as I had gone. (4)

We know that our will power alone initially isn't able to set us free. Our disabling attachments are more forceful than the power of our wills. Our will is essentially useless initially as we begin the first part of our recovery program. Bill W.., explains how this is and what is needed if we are to become free again. Bill W.., tells his story: ... my friend sat before me, and he made the point blank declaration that God had done for him what he could not do for himself. His human will had failed. Doctors had pronounced him incurable. Society was indeed about to lock him up.

Like myself, he had admitted complete defeat. Then he had, in effect, been raised from the dead and suddenly taken from the scrap heap to a level of life better than the best he had ever known! Had this power originated in him? Obviously it had not. There had been no more power in him than there was in me at that minute, and this was none at all. That floored me. It began to look as though religious people were right after all. Here was something at work in human hearts which had done the impossible. My ideas about miracles were drastically revised right then. Never mind the musty past; here sat a miracle directly across the kitchen table. He shouted great tidings. (4) But you might say, 'I thought that depression was all about a chemical imbalance, a hormonal shift, or even worse, a mental illness. I never had an inkling that my depression had anything to do with the way we create meaning for one's life or our life's experiences.

We know that for many of us in the fellowship that our depression has been a continued scourge since childhood and medication has been the mainstay of some sort of pain relief. A fellowship of the spirit has never been a conscious option for many of us who were depressed. We didn't have a clue that we even had a chance to leave our isolated depression prison. Little has been told how we might want to seek alternative and adjunctive directions for relief from our pain.

Bill W.., continues this thought when he writes:
It was only a matter of being willing to believe in a power greater than myself. Nothing more was required of me to make a beginning. I saw that growth could start from that point. Upon a foundation of complete willingness I might build what I saw in my friend. Would I have it? Of course I would. (4)

This is the alternative for all of us who have tried everything to ease our pain and isolation. We have tried the drugs; we have tried the therapies and read all the self-help books ever written on the subject of depression. And still to this day we continue to struggle against the deadly demon of darkness.

Bill W.., continues: ....Common sense would thus become uncommon sense. I was to sit quietly when in doubt, asking only for direction and strength to meet my problems as He would have me.

Never was I to pray for myself, except as my requests bore on my usefulness to others. Then only might I expect to receive. But that would be in great measure. (4)

He states that
My friend promised when these things were done I would enter upon a new relationship with my Creator; that I would have the elements of a way of living which answered all my problems. Belief in the power of God, plus enough willingness, honesty and humility to establish and maintain the new order of things, were the essential requirements. Simple, but not easy; a price had to be paid. It meant destruction of self-centeredness. I must turn in all things to the Father of Light who presides over us all. (2)

Bill W.., stresses the essential relationship between recovery from our debilitating attachments and the necessity of having a vital spiritual awakening. It's about establishing a relationship with a Power Greater than just ourselves. We believe that in order for any of us to grow to maturity and freedom from sadness there are things we have to do and which has to do with this spiritual reality of being connected to the god of our understanding.

My friend had emphasized the absolute necessity of demonstrating these principles in all my affairs, particularly was it imperative to work with others as he had worked with me. Faith without works is dead, he said. And how appallingly true for the alcoholic! For if an alcoholic failed to perfect and enlarge his spiritual life through work and self-sacrifice for others, he could not survive the certain trials and low spots ahead... (4)

I find the insights of Bill W., to be at the cutting edge of whether or not a person depressed gets better or just simply gets, i.e., gets more isolated and disconnected from life. It is difficult for the newcomer to believe that it will have to take some time before they can feel the positive effects of this program of hope. Depressed Anonymous provides that necessary atmosphere of hope and a new beginning. How often have we patiently waited for the drugs prescribed by our doctors to take effect? We know that drugs taken to deal with our depression can work well, work for a while or not work at all. And when the drugs that are prescribed for depression fail to work we know how discouraging that becomes.

But the fellowship of the group can be found to work its healing and restoration as we attend more and more meetings.

As many members of our fellowship has stated "they now know that their depression did not just come out of the blue." They gradually come to realize that their pain originates from within themselves and that the spiritual principles of the 12 Steps can help lead them to the source of their pain. The painful sadness which begins gradually as a small unseen seed began to be nurtured unconsciously by our own life choices and decisions. These choices became a weight which overwhelmed my mind and my spirit. My life became unmanageable. I had to admit, finally, that I was powerless over something that began to have a life of its own and whose direction I was no longer the master. Looking back over my life and this experience I discovered that my thoughts produce beliefs, the beliefs produce feelings and feelings produce moods and moods produce behavior. The mind- body connection is never as much in evidence as it is in this human experience which we label depression. Many times the seeds of our present depression have been planted unconsciously and may stem back to days of our childhood. As we have said before, and which bears repeating, it is only when we grow into adulthood that these unconscious or "implicit memories" as they are called, get triggered by present difficult circumstances. These memories become conscious and are then labeled "explicit memories." These memories help us re-experience outdated and forgotten abandonment's, losses, some un-grieved, from many years back. Even though forgotten, these memories are not gone from our consciousness.

So often a child has some preverbal images of one's primary caregiver where the infant as a child might have felt abandoned – not loved, but even now, this person in their present adult life has situations and events that can trigger and uncover old and unconscious painful emotions. Some of those early frightening childhood scenes can be reactivated and brought to present light by spouse, employer, lover, or friend. These frightening images send us back to the safety of the familiar and the predictable – the comfort of our depression.

How strange to call such a horrific feeling, a potentially life threatening feeling, a comfort. But some of us who have been depressed do just that. At least we know what we got. The feeling is predictable. Who knows, if we change anything in our lives we might just get something far worse. It's better to have something we know than to risk getting something worse. Since we know that change can be frightening – the depressed thinks why take the chance and try to change? It's much like knowing that we need to see the dentist for a bothersome toothache – but foreseeing pain, we would rather have the toothache than get something that we believe would be much worse.

This event is the cause that keeps us ruminating over and over again and with it the concomitant unpleasant feelings that continue to work their negative and harmful effects on our mind, body & spirit. They are still around – like an unborn child kicking inside a mother's womb – waiting to see the light of day. These feelings are attached to one's psyche like the proverbial tick on a dog's back. For those of us who are depressed or who have been depressed, we find that the light of day can be brought about by being an active participant in Depressed Anonymous the 12 step fellowship.

I knew if could have had one good day or a lifetime of good days before my own depression then I knew that it made sense that I could have a good day again. And so to continue my own story, I knew that whatever had me by the throat I still needed to keep motivating myself every day to keep acting on my own behalf.

Many hurting folks come to Depressed Anonymous with the mistaken belief that they are coming to a class; while there, someone will teach them how to quickly, that is, translated "painlessly" and get them out of their depression. They want a quick fix and so hurry back to living the way they used to live. And all this without any conscious effort to discover what got them depressed in the first place. They may fail to realize that they have to do some work on themselves if they want to stay free from relapse. There is no talk of a quick fix in the Depressed Anonymous fellowship – there are no magic pills, and no magic wands which someone wafts over our head and suddenly, presto! we are feeling brand new! No, in our program, normally time has to pass and we will have to have a "vital spiritual experience" which gets us committed to something bigger than ourselves. And that vital spiritual experience can be the support received from the mutual aid support of Depressed Anonymous.

Bill W states a truth when he states that during acute depression, avoid trying to set your whole life in order all at once. If you take on assignments so heavy that you are sure to fail in them at the moment, then you are allowing yourself to be tricked by your unconscious. Thus you will continue to make sure of your failure, and when it comes you will have another alibi for still more retreat into depression.

In short, the 'all or nothing' attitude is a most destructive one. It is best to begin with whatever the irreducible minimums of activity are. Then work for an enlargement of these – day by day. Don't be disconcerted by setbacks – just start over. (2)

In Depressed Anonymous we soon learn that to get well we have to believe that we are not passive victims of depression which comes out of the blue and bites us. We are not talking about cold and flu here. We learn that to be responsible for our own health and healing. We have to learn that **MOTIVATION FOLLOWS ACTION**. I will not blame myself for being depressed but ***I do have to take responsibility*** for my own health now that I know what I have. We are responsible for the depression in the fact that it resides and has its home in us and has crippled us for months, and yes, possibly even years. Now that we have provided hope with a step by step recovery program we think it possible to use our program, attend our meetings, read our literature and take life as it comes – one day at a time.

In our meetings we learn how to take responsibility for our own feelings and health. We know how to do the "next right thing and move on." It would be well for us to take a look at our early life relationships, especially what life was like in our early childhood years and in our early life relationships. It is very important to examine our early life experiences and relationships. Were we loved? Were we cherished by our parents? Was there drinking in the home? Was there abuse? Were we ignored? Were we allowed to experience life outside the boundaries of our own home? Were we able to see that life was large and that we were part of this life? Did we believe that we were valued as a human person?

If you had parents who said you were worthless and unsuitable and were no good then this has without doubt influenced you in deep and painful ways even to this day. To feel worthless and unacceptable is truly one of the greatest pains that a person can experience.

If you have seen the movie <u>Goodwill Hunting</u>? You have to be moved by this tragic story which illustrates too well what happens to those who were abused when young and because they were led to believe they are unacceptable and worthless they look in all the wrong directions and with the wrong people for affirmation and validation.

Bill W.., knows all too well the pain that we feel and the price that we have paid for our addictions and negative attachments. Many times, in our own recovery we find ourselves slipping back into old feelings and harmful patterns of thinking and behaving. And of course one of our worst enemies is a desire to isolate and hide.

Bill W.., says that
When I am feeling depressed, I repeat to myself statements such as these: "pain is the touchstone of

progress"...."Fear no evil"...This too will pass"..."This experience can be turned to benefit."

    These fragments of prayer bring far more than mere comfort. They keep me on the track of right acceptance; they break up my compulsive themes of guilt, depression, rebellion, and pride; and sometimes they endow me with the courage to change the things I can, and the wisdom to know the difference. (2)

    Also, we know that one major manifestation of depression is what is called Obsessive Compulsive behavior – that ritualistic attempt to reduce stress by repetitive rituals such as hand washing or checking doors and stove burners. Also OCD affects thoughts in that they too become obsessive. All of this is a persons' ritualistic attempt at reducing stress. Allied with this disability is perfectionism where a person who is obsessive /compulsive has a hyper moral sensitivity. Everything has to be perfect. No mistakes allowed!

    We also learn that our depression is a defense and predictable and for some, depression is even come to be a comfort and as has been said before, at least one knows what they have with depression. And to change and risk removing this numbness is better not to be undertaken because it's better to know what one has than to risk getting something worse. Much like the example cited before of the debate within ourselves to go to the dentist for the toothache or just tough it out and hope for the best. We call this denial.

    When the depressed person starts to feel a bit better the thought immediately springs up that this new and good feeling won't last. This self-fulfilling prophecy takes over and we live out our own desires. We can't risk getting better – that means major changes – painful changes. But as we get sick and tired of being sick and tired of our pain we begin to go to work on ourselves (like now, as you continue to read this book) even though the depressed person believes that since bad things happened in the past that bad things will continue to happen in the future. They believe there "is no chance for me to get better."

Now I have to dig in and dismember those core beliefs that keep us repeating the same thinking, the same behavior which can keep us imprisoned in our depression. We have this compulsion to repeat – this ritual of defeat – because, first of all it is comfortable and secondly it keeps us from having to do something different, namely something that we haven't done before. We continue to move round in a circle always meeting up with the same me – no major changes evident. If we don't start the process of change, then not without surprise our life then stays the same. But this also closes the doors to the future and with it a sense of hope and relief. It seems that to believe that we have no future and that we will always feel this way can imprison us as we empower these absolute beliefs that nothing good will ever happen for us. We are thus chained to our own self will and not only are we imprisoned but we are the jailer as well. The key is in our hands and it is there for the asking.

Bill W.., speaks hope when he tells how it was the prayer of St. Francis that was the key in unlocking his dependence upon depression.
I asked myself, "Why can't the Twelve Steps work to release me from this unbearable depression?" By the

hour, I stared at the St. Francis Prayer: "It is better to comfort than to be comforted."

Suddenly I realized what the answer might be. My basic flaw had always been dependence on people or circumstances to supply me with prestige, security, and confidence. Failing to get these things according to my need to be perfect with my own dreams and desires, I fought for them. And when defeat came, so did my depression.

Reinforced by what grace I could find in prayer, I had to exert every ounce of will and action to cut off these faulty emotional dependencies upon people and upon circumstances. Then only could I be free to love as Francis had loved. (2)

It is my conviction now (after many years of one or two meetings a week with depressed groups plus my own clinical practice of more than 20 years) that people who keep coming back to a Depressed Anonymous meeting are more apt to get better.

Those that keep working the program, day after day and with the recovery tools gained from frequent Depressed Anonymous meetings, these active members of the fellowship find life and a circle of friends who are now a big part of one's healing. That's a promise in Alcoholics Anonymous and it is a promise that is true for all 12 step fellowships including our Depressed Anonymous. I've been witness to it. Our program is not an easy one but it is a simple one. We have a solution. And as the saying goes, "If you want something that you never had before, then you must do something that you never did before."

A personal testimony in the Alcoholics Anonymous Big Book makes the following powerful statement that I realize that all I'm guaranteed in life is today. The poorest person has no less and the wealthiest has no more – each of us has but one day.

What we do with it is our own business; how we use it is up to us individually. I feel that I have been restored to health and sanity these past years not through my own efforts nor as a result of anything I may have done, but because I've come to believe – to really believe-that alone I can do nothing. That my own innate selfishness and stubbornness are the evils which, if left unguarded, can drive me to alcohol. I have come to believe that my illness is spiritual as well as physical and mental, and I know that for help in the spiritual sphere I have to turn to a Higher Power. (4)

And again, Bill tells us
We had to quit playing God. It didn't work. We decided that hereafter, in this drama of life; God was going to be our Director. He would be the Principal; we, his agents. Most good ideas are simple, and this concept was the keystone of the new triumphal arch through which we passed to freedom. (2)

And in another place he says

Beyond a Higher Power, as each of us may vision him, AA (DA as well) must never, as a society, enter the field of dogma or theology. We can never become a religion in that sense, lest we kill our usefulness by getting bogged down in theological contention. (2)

And it's the spiritual awakening that finally moves us out into the world toward those still suffering. Having had a spiritual awakening as the result of these steps, we tried to carry this message to the depressed, and to practice these principles in all of our affairs. (3)

We have all learned that by giving help and support to others "still suffering from depression" that our own suffering and pain is diminished and finally can be eradicated. And so we are grateful to you, Bill W., for your words which continue to provide healing to this very day. Your own brokenness and road to restoration has been the restoration for thousands of those who once were broken and now living lives of hope and serenity.

CHAPTER THREE

WHAT IS DEPRESSED ANONYMOUS?

Depressed Anonymous is modeled after the 12 steps (principles) of Alcoholics Anonymous and was founded in Evansville, Indiana in May of 1985. It uses a group approach where members mutually support each other.

In DEPRESSED ANONYMOUS the depressed person admits that he/she is powerless over his or her depression. The depressed person admits that the various areas of his/her life are controlled by depression, and that he/she needs help from one's inner resources, combined with a faith in a Higher Power to help work through one's time of hopelessness and helplessness.

At Depressed Anonymous meetings, we do not pry into people's personal lives. We also do not give advice at meetings but instead tell our own story and how the 12 steps are releasing us from the tight grip of depression. Meetings are normally upbeat and the focus is positive! Each of us set small concrete and positive goals for ourselves and begin to learn how to gain some mastery over our lives and feelings. Each of us has time at meetings to share our experiences with other members of the group. As a new member you are ready to make a commitment to quit sadding oneself, and that's when results begin to happen. This 12 step recovery program can be a great healer of personal wounds and provides the depressed with a new start in life. It also provides hope for people like yourself who have been where you are. Hope

I'LL DO IT WHEN I FEEL BETTER

now resides where once there was only darkness and despair!

You may choose someone to help you stick to this plan. This person is called a sponsor and should be someone who has experienced depression themselves and presently is using the spiritual principles of the 12 steps for their own recovery. You can also exchange phone numbers with other members of the DA group. As life gets better for you and the emotional pain gets less and you are no longer experiencing isolation you can use your past experiences in helping the new members of the DA group see that there truly is a way out of their prison of depression. You have already learned what Bill W., experienced personally that if you want healing then you must be a healer for others.

THE AIMS OF DEPRESSED ANONYMOUS:

- To let the depressed person know that she or he is not alone in his or her struggle with depression. We also help others learn to do pleasant activities again.
- To provide a group where members can help one another and learn new skills in taking mastery over their lives and begin to live again with hope and joy.
- To help each member feel better about themselves – today. One day at a time!
- To educate the depressed person and his or her family about the nature and causes of depression and remove the SHAME of their feeling depressed. It's OK to admit that we are feeling overwhelmed.

That taught me the most important lesson I have ever learned in my entire life. That is that AA doesn't need me, but I need AA. Very desperately, very sincerely, very humbly. Not all at once, because you can't ever get it all at once, just a little bit at a time. They told me, "You've got to get out and work a little, you've got to give. "They told me that giving was living, and living was loving, and loving was God. And you don't have to worry about God, because He's sitting right in front of your eyes. (4)

AND MORE ABOUT DEPRESSION

The experience of depression is the experience of the effects of isolation, of living in a frightening and dangerous world. In this century many people have had this kind of experience in the course of long-term imprisonment in solitary confinement and some of their numbers have attempted to describe not only what happened to them but also what stratagems they devised for survival. Cohen and Taylor recently surveyed the studies of psychological survival and concluded that "repeated affirmation by survivors suggests the first rule of any handbook on survival: understand what is happening to you. (5)

Depression as a set of symptoms, which are called a syndrome in clinical speech and are affecting persons of every nationality and creed worldwide. The World Health Organization said that because of <u>cultural disparity, cultural disintegration</u>, immigration and <u>universal homelessness</u> that because of these and <u>family breakdown</u>, by reason of <u>divorce</u> and <u>smaller family units</u> all these have played a part in a global mental health problem. Depression as has been pointed out is a complexity of symptoms, from loss of weight, gaining weight, insomnia and sleeping too much. And among other symptoms in our particular view of depression, our mentor Dr. Rowe pointed out in her many studies that depression produces some absolute beliefs for those suffering from depression.

In the work Depressed Anonymous, which provides a step by step commentary for individual and group members, Dr. Rowe points out that if you want to get yourself depressed this is what you must do. You must hold these six opinions as if they were real, absolute, and immutable Truths.

1) No matter how good and nice I appear to be, I am really bad, evil, valueless, and unacceptable to myself and others.
2) Other people are such that I must fear, hate and envy them.
3) Life is terrible and death is worse.
4) Only bad things happened to me in the past and only bad things will happen to me in the future.
5) Anger is evil.
6) I must never forgive, least of all myself. (6)

What I envision as the best possible world for the depressed and to prevent relapse and recurrence is a model that includes the medication treatment, the psychotherapy interaction between therapist and client and then the holistic model of the mutual aid group. What happens in the group support system is basically a replication of what happens in a person's childhood environment. We can determine if trust is there, can the child have the assumed permission to show initiative, is the child made to feel safe and can the child venture out beyond the boundaries of his home and feel safe. Or does he come from a home which is closed and the world perceived as enemy and unsafe--indeed a setup for a mistrustful attitude about life – all this comes into play in early child development. We need to look again at anything in a child's life where he/she experienced a loss, a separation or a life filled with anger and hurt.

The community in which the child is raised presents all types of messages and this in the beginning is how he or she sees the world. Chemicals in the brain don't produce thoughts that say, "I'm worthless or unacceptable, etc. It's more the messages that one receives when one is in the formative years of one's life that may predict how one perceives his or her future.

The following is Fred's story from AA and how the spirituality of the Alcoholics Anonymous program, much like that of Depressed Anonymous came to save him from the darkness of despair into the light of hope. Quite as important was the discovery that spiritual principles would solve all my problems. I have since been brought into a way of living infinitely more satisfying and, I hope, more useful than the life I lived before. My old manner of life was by no means a bad one, but I would not exchange its best moments for the worst I have now. I would not go back to it even I could. (4)

You might find it helpful to answer the following questions:

Whom do you feel responsible for? In what ways do these people need you? What would happen if you didn't meet their needs? How do you feel? You but you fail to help them? In what ways have you lost some of your identity by feeling, thinking, and acting the way others want you to feel, think and act? What aspects of your own life have you neglected as you have focused on the needs of others (consider emotional health, physical health, financial well-being, your schedule, relationships, relaxation, fun)?

    The final word here is that one's own renewed and restored sane thinking can and will manifest in behaviors that not only produce sanity and healing but will also give one the strength to share one's own story – the before and the after with those "still suffering from depression."

CHAPTER FOUR

THE PROMISES OF DEPRESSED ANONYMOUS

PART ONE

In Alcoholics Anonymous we first read about what the Promises are as they appear originally in Alcoholics Anonymous, and now quoted verbatim in Depressed Anonymous. (3)

Both you and the new man (woman) must walk day by day in the path of spiritual progress. If you persist, remarkable things will happen. When we look back, we realize that the things, which came to us when we put ourselves in God's hands, were better than anything we could have planned. Follow the dictates of a Higher Power and you will presently live in a new and wonderful world, no matter what your present circumstances." (3)

And

If we are painstaking about this phase of our development, we will be amazed before we are halfway through. We are going to know a new happiness. We will not regret the past nor wish to shut the door on it. We will comprehend the word serenity and we will know peace. No matter how far down the scale we have gone, we will see how our experience can benefit others. That feeling of uselessness and self-pity will disappear. We will lose interest in selfish things and gain interest in our fellows. Self-seeking will slip away. Our whole attitude and outlook upon life will change. Fear of people and of economic insecurity will leave us. We will intuitively know how to handle situations, which used to baffle us. We will suddenly realize that God is doing for us what we could not do for ourselves.

Are these extravagant promises? We think not. They are being fulfilled among us – sometimes quickly, sometimes slowly. They will always materialize if we work for them." (3)

The promises, the gifts we receive offer much hard work. The light at the end of the tunnel, the gold at the end of the rainbow. It always helps to have some idea of where your recovery work is going to lead you. The promises serve as a way to measure how far one has come and how far you have to go. (19)

Now let's look at the Promises as they have been organized into 13 separate statements by the fellowship of Depressed Anonymous.

This is the place where we can start to reflect upon what these promises are about. The promises were originally lists on page 83-84 of the Big Book of Alcoholics Anonymous. In Depressed Anonymous, they appear in the last chapter, which deals with Step 12. In essence, we see that after you have begun to work the steps, actually the majority of them you will begin to see some areas of your life changing. There is a new awareness – a new consciousness that awakens in your spirit. You have already said that you believe in a power greater than yourself. You've by now made a decision to turn your life and your will over to god and made a good effort to clean house and begin to take responsibility for your life.

As we go to our meetings, work the steps (see the Depressed Anonymous Workbook, DAP, 2002.) and talk to others in our recovery group, we begin to find that our work is beginning to pay off. We are indeed something new – it is indeed like we have been reborn. (7)

We know that 1) Depressed Anonymous educates and informs us about our experience of depression. 2) We know that depressed Anonymous nurtures us so that we can begin to share unashamedly our unpleasant feelings with others. 3) Depressed Anonymous accepts us and does not make judgments about our experience with depression. In other words we don't hear snap out of it from the members of the fellowship. 4) Depressed Anonymous teaches coping skills by our frequent meetings and group membership interaction. We know about being connected with like-minded folks. Depressed Anonymous empowers us so that we feel there is truly a way out of depression for self and /or my loved ones. One of the major benefits of the group is that you can hear how other persons depressed have made it out of their depression. It also is clear that the program works best for those who keep coming back to the meetings. We say come to at least six meetings and if you are not feeling differently we guarantee your misery back.

It is our wonderful and personal experience to witness how those who keep coming back to meetings week after week start to look more relaxed and happier... and many of these are persons who have been depressed from childhood. You can't help but being a believer when you witness others gradually freeing themselves from depression.

Having the belief that you can get better is what in time can free you from your depression. Is this a wild promise without a basis in reality? No, the program really does work and we are not trying to raise false hopes. We know that our program takes work – in time you will be able to free yourself from depression.

THE PROMISES

1. IF WE ARE PAINSTAKING ABOUT THIS PHASE OF OUR DEVELOPMENT WE WILL BE AMAZED BEFORE WE ARE HALFWAY THROUGH.

Change is painful. The first step is really the beginning of the end of our pain. By admitting that we are in pain is that which paradoxically begins the release of our pain. This is the paradox of letting go and holding on as we learned from Step Three. _What we hold onto holds onto us._ What we seek – seeks us.

This pain of depression begins to dissolve as a result of doing something we have never done before- or rather doing something about our lives that we have not done before. It happens to be true that the more we get in touch with and remove our resentments, fear, guilt and self-pity from our lives, the lighter we feel emotionally. The less need we have to rely on our defense mechanisms, which shielded our fragile egos from pain, hurt, or remorse, the freer we become.

I believe that the pain of our depression originates from inside us. We construct present day reality based on past life experiences. The past is a predictor of the future.

As it says in Depressed Anonymous, many of us held the absolute belief that "since bad things have happened to us in the past bad things will happen to us in the future." In other words we have made up our minds-nothing will ever change. And of course this belief is what promotes and keeps our depression alive.

The opposite of depression is spontaneity and vitality. When we are depressed we move about as in a fog. We are stuck. Since we desire everything to remain the same and predictable, we are unable to believe that life is or can be different. As we change old beliefs into new ones we believe that things can change as things begin to change. We will begin to experience hope, light and joy.

Remember, by the time you have reached the promises in the Big Book of AA, page 64, you have decided to do something about your life. You not only have been through an exhaustive self-examination of your life but you will also have shared these experiences with another human being by working Step Five. You have taken the time and the pain to write down all those areas of your life which have kept you in the dark-not only about yourself, but all that your life could be.

Bill W.., tells us that "when pain comes, we are expected to learn from it willingly, and help others to learn. When happiness comes, we accept it as a gift and thank god for it...

In every AA story (DA) pain has been the process of admission into a new life. But the admission price purchased more than we expected. It led us to a measure of humility, which we soon discovered to be a healer of pain. We began to fear pain less, and desire humility more than ever. (18)

In Depressed Anonymous we read

The god that we know speaks to us through members of the Depressed Anonymous group. The Higher Power will put a new sense of purpose into your life once you know how to turn to it and surrender your pain. The Depressed Anonymous group will lead you safely and gently. The miracle is in the group.

The starting point is the admission that so far everything we have tried has not worked... (3)

"...Life doesn't have to be lived alone in agony or misery." (3)

2. WE REALIZE A NEW WAY TO LIVE.

After having made a clean breast of things we begin to live with a clean conscience. We have made amends, made it right with our god, others and ourselves.

How does one acquire freedom? Freedom is based on detachment. Detachment means to no longer cling to persons, places, things or behavior that cripples or demeans itself or others.

In our struggle with depression, we had felt that we had lost all freedom and happiness. We now know that we have the key to our prison in our hands and as we move through each of the steps a new fact was discovered, that we don't have to remain frozen in time with our depression. We know that now we can celebrate a release from all the old fears, resentments and images that we held of ourselves over these many years.

Our happiness is now dependent on how we look at ourselves, our world and the understanding that we have of our God. I know for a fact that when I first came into the fellowship, I felt like a stranger in a foreign country. My thoughts and feelings were all confused as I began the journey into myself with a deepening desire to discover the engine that drives my sadness. The battle raged inside of me – a battle that was fought in the shadow of a past event (s) – relationship(s). It was a personal triumph for me to finally see that there was a way out of this despair and emotional atrophy. I feel that my life got better by my doing something. I now follow a practical plan as outlined by our suggested 12-step program. I make sure that every day that I get into action and do something. I used to think that if I wait long enough the good humor fairy would tap me on the shoulder and I would be well. This is exactly the opposite of what our program of recovery promotes. Our position is that you have to roll up your sleeves and get to work.

A pill might make you feel differently-but it will never take away the circumstances that brought you down in the first place. The Promises here tell us that we will find a new freedom of happiness-but first work has to be done. Our lives and the way we look at life are composed of past and present events.

3. WE DO NOT REGRET THE PAST NOR WISH TO SHUT THE DOOR ON IT.

This does not mean that "oh well, we made some mistakes so let's just forget about everything that happened in the past-after all it's in the past."

We can spend a lot of wasted time wallowing in the self-pity that occupies any addiction. We also might regret all the time that we wasted staring at the blank wall, alone and trying to figure out in the circling of our thoughts the why of our immobility, passivity and pain.

It is in steps four and five where our past regrets are played out and dealt with. Once we have made a list (Step four) of all our resentments and fears and spoke of them to a trusted friend (Step five) we can begin to feel a new sense of freedom.

When we suppress a negative emotion and refuse to deal with it, either consciously or unconsciously, it becomes one of those blocks that form the walls of our personal prison. These unexpressed emotions can fester and boil over so that our energy level is dissipated, scattered. We find ourselves and our will enervated and weakened. We discover that with the internal war raging inside of us we can hardly find the energy to get to work and /or roll ourselves out of bed a morning. The pain of depression freezes all efforts at mobility. We no longer have the freeing feeling of spontaneity in our lives.

We discover that our ability to make ourselves do something is now beyond our personal strength and power. We have become helpless.

We also discover that we are powerless. Our will power has no control over this depression.

But how do we know this particular promise will come true for me? What we can rely on is our own experiences. Our experiences tell us that the more we live in the <u>solution of the promises</u> of Depressed Anonymous the more serenity and peace will be ours. We have discovered that it is when we begin to live in the <u>solution and not focus on our problems that will</u> lead us past the fear of what might happen to the serenity of the present moment. We no longer wait with trepidation for the other shoe to drop. Our freedom begins when we start to reflect consciously on what is happening now at this very moment. I have noticed that it is when I became conscious about what I am feeling now is the direct result of my thinking which enables me to make the conscious decision to bring myself back to the present.

4. WE COMPREHEND THE W0RD SERENITY AND WE KNOW PEACE OF MIND.

Agitations, anxiety and jitteriness were all part of my life as I muddled through day after day, one foot in front of the other. Serenity was definitely not a part of my life.

As with any attachment to a negative behavior, serenity and peace was the farthest thing from my life. The new beliefs and thoughts which I heard expressed at Depressed Anonymous meetings started to help me change the way I thought about myself, my world and my future.

I believe that it takes work, time and prayer and quiet periods of meditation to achieve the peace and serenity that we are talking about here.

Peace of mind is the result of:

1) A clear conscience
2) Living in the present
3) Gratitude everyday
4) Belief that the God of my understanding will get me through the problems of my life
5) Forgiveness of myself and amends to all person I have harmed
6) Hope
7) Doing God's will means letting go.

I am firmly convinced that in order to continue any semblance of peace and serenity I will have to structure a daily quiet period into my life. This is an essential part of the prescription for getting well and staying well.

Also, I believe that when I am quiet, God can give to me all that is mine to have. My will and my life have to be attuned to God's presence and love. We will know that in order for God to make itself present to us and demonstrate its love we have to sit still, be quiet and listen with purity of heart. This is an essential part of the formula where we will find our sobriety and serenity.

It is my belief that God does speak to those who remain quiet and have a desire to listen. Peace is defined as "an undisturbed state of mind, absence of mental conflict." Serenity is defined as "a quality or state of being serene; calmness; tranquility."

The quality or state of being serene all takes time, work and discipline. I believe that the big book of AA says it best: When we sincerely took such a position, all sorts of remarkable things followed. We had a new employer; being all-powerful he provided what we needed, if we kept close to him and performed his work well. Established on such a footing we became less and less interested in plans, our little designs and ourselves. More and more we became interested in seeing what we could contribute to life. As we felt new power flow in, as we enjoyed peace of mind, as we discovered we could face life successfully, as we became conscious of his presence, we began to lose our fear of today, tomorrow or the hereafter. We're reborn. (4)

This particular section following step two declares that we "came to believe that a power greater than ourselves could restore us to sanity." This is an important part of our getting re-centered and renewed as we let the power flow into our lives.
...We may have had certain spiritual beliefs, but now we begin to have a spiritual experience.... We feel that we are on the Broad Highway walking hand in hand with the Spirit of this Universe.

"Both you and the new man must walk day by day in the path of spiritual progress. If you persist we believe remarkable things will happen. When we look back, we realize that the things, which came to us when we put ourselves in god's hands, were better than anything we could have planned. Follow the dictates of a Higher Power and you will presently live in a new and wonderful world, no matter what your present circumstances. (4)

5. NO MATTER HOW FAR DOWN THE SCALE WE HAVE GONE, WE SEE HOW OUR EXPERIENCE CAN BENEFIT OTHERS.

Some of us have attempted suicide. A few of us more than a few times. We had despaired of ever finding peace or hope. We believed that we had no future and that our yesterdays were as hopeless as our today's. It was hard to attend our first Depressed Anonymous meeting. We felt horribly alone. We just know that no one in the group has been through what we had been through. But as we listened and watched the older members of the group speak we saw ourselves in their stories.

Personally, I believe that whatever you give out to others is the amount that comes back to you. Our experience can usually help someone else. As the experience of depression is so isolating, so predictable in its misery that it is bound to have made such impression upon us that it changed our life and the way we think about our life. And then when our life is changed for the better – thanks to the fellowship of DA, this precious gift of hope needs to be with those still suffering. Ironically, it appears that the farther we have gone down in mood-and up again in our recovery the more powerful can this experience be.

New members of our fellowship see the "after" of our lives lived in recovery and so they themselves get involved in the fellowship. The fact that we have recovered so completely is in itself a message of tremendous hope for those who are newcomers to the group. Isn't it amazing that those who can do the most for those still suffering are those who have worked themselves out of the pit of isolation and begin sharing their story of hope and personal empowerment.

CHAPTER FIVE

THE PROMISES OF DEPRESSED ANONYMOUS

PART TWO

6. THE FEELINGS OF USELESSNESS AND SELF-PITY DISAPPEAR.

One of the major areas in our lives that change quickly by our attendance at the group meetings is that we pity ourselves less and less. We begin to be grateful for all that we have and all that we are. We begin to see that once we start getting connected to others like ourselves on a regular basis, through our Depressed Anonymous meetings, we now are listened to by others and we are validated. We don't hear "snap out of it" at our meetings. Suddenly our years of self-pity, isolation and desolation have been cashed in for a currency that buys us a new competency, a new identity, autonomy and a burgeoning inter relatedness with others. We know we are not alone.

We now can speak about our experience with depression in the past tense. We now can share how we have the tools of self-care whereby we can dig out and begin to construct an edifice of hope that will last the rest of our lives. As long as we continue to use the tools of the program we are bound to feel different as well as think differently.

We know that self-pity promotes a greater attention to the problem, while attention to how our experience may help others promotes not only our own well-being but that of others as well.

We learn how the program works, and this happens primarily by attending meetings. The solutions and ideas presented at all our meetings help us all to become more active in the pursuit of our own serenity as promised by the fellowship.

When we were depressing ourselves we felt not only useless, but also unacceptable to ourselves and to others. It seems that the harder we pushed to fight against depression the sadder we became.

When we begin to feel differently we also begin to believe differently. We learn how to become more hopeful and helpful.

Why do I continue the work of bringing hope to those still suffering? What motivates me to continue to try and help others? What has made the change in my life where now I want to share what I know and how I feel? Basically, I know that the program of recovery works. I no longer feel powerless over my depression. . In DA group meetings members speak my language. We see how useless it is to waste time looking back over our shoulder to see if the dark shadow of my own inner fears is going to overtake me. I now have attained small amounts of hope and strength as I go from day to day. I am prepared for those moments of despair that at times overtake me and cause me to feel paralyzed and out of control.

In the first step "we admitted we were powerless over depression and that our lives had become unmanageable." It is a paradox that it is in the admission that our lives are out of control that we begin to take control of our lives.

7. WE HAVE LESS CONCERN ABOUT SELF AND GAIN INTEREST IN OTHERS

OTHERS

As we start our program of recovery we notice that there are persons in the group who are less well off than are we.

Newcomers also remind us of ourselves when we stepped into the group for the first time. They struggle to keep back tears and hurt as they speak, possibly for the first time trusting that they are with people who have been where they are. This is what provides the beginning of hope and healing.
People in the group speak their language of hope and possibility. They hear how recovery is possible. They want those tools to use in their own recovery.
...We need to air our hurts, our shame, and let others hear our story. (3)

It is almost a truism to say about those of us who want this program, are not now focused on self but on the will of God for our lives. I personally believe that once I have made the first step, and admitted my powerlessness, I set in motion a force, a loving force of the creator in my personal life. In time I am filled with energy and find that this power can change me and restore my life with purpose and meaning. It can prepare me to meet those who are willing to risk leaving the prison of their depression. By my own interest in getting in touch with the Higher Power and getting its direction to "do the next right thing" I find that my own life is gradually becoming more filled with purpose and energy.

There is a saying that to gain energy you must give energy. I have found this to be true for my own life.

What appears to deplete our energy is when our thoughts implode and collide with each other, as they are kept focused on the problem. If you nurture yourself, you will find that just as in the natural world, the growth will be good and the growth will be gradual. We learn that there are no quick fixes in life just solutions that will result with time and work.

We all have a competence, an identity, autonomy and interrelatedness to everything alive around us. We are truly a part of every living community on the planet and in this entire universe. We are all one. The more we see ourselves as part and parcel of this universe then nothing can prevent us from feeling that we have every right to be here.

I know that as I prepare my daily life with prayer and meditation that my self-seeking will disappear. I will want to share with those still suffering from depression that hope is very possible for them just as it is for me. The more you and I wait on God's still small voice in our daily times of quiet we find that God begins to move you into its plan and prepare for you and guide you to execute its will where you live. God has a plan for each of us, and the power of its will can free us from ourselves, our worst fears and into the solution of freedom. We want to stick to the plan.

Joel Goldsmith a spiritual writer contends that the more we gain this consciousness of god's presence you have the whole secret of success in every walk of life." page 145

Goldsmith said

"There is an invisible bond between all of us. We are not on earth to get from one another, but to share those spiritual treasures which are of god. Our interest in each other is, in truth, purely spiritual. Our purpose in life is the unfolding of the spirit within." Page 146

As Bill W states in the AA Big Book,

...we let god demonstrate through us, what god can do. We ask god to remove our fear and direct our attention to what god would have us be. At once, we commence to outgrow fear. (4)

We believe that as we become aware that god dwells in each of us and demonstrates its power in us the more we remain open to God's presence.

We humans are so grounded in the material and the spatial that it is veritably impossible to be conscious of a higher power in and around us. We now believe that we can tap into this God consciousness and let it unfold its plan, its purpose and mission for our life. It will not plan something small and insignificant but will, by small steps, lead us, cause to unfold in our lives what it has for us to accomplish. And I believe the spiritual nature and the fellowship of Depressed Anonymous is what god uses to get us aware and conscious of its love and presence.

8. OUR WHOLE OUTLOOK AND ATTITUDE UPON LIFE CHANGES.

To really believe, possibly for the first time in one's life that I can free myself from the prison of depression and begin to feel better. I know that I need to be proactive in my efforts at self-recovery. But what causes our outlook and attitude to change?

I have to begin to believe that hope and healing is possible. Once we have gone through some painful inner changes, such as dealing with our character defects and our isolating tendencies we see there is a way out. We have to have a positive attitude that will move and motivate us to want to go and get to the next step. Watching someone actually take these steps week after week and watch that feeling of wellness rise up in them can promote a belief that with work and time, their lives do improve. Soon we see that a <u>sense of purpose</u> begins to manifest itself the more time and work we put into our personal recovery.

A door opens ever slightly, and there appears a potential route to freedom. A way out! I do know that when my hope and faith in recovery rises, my symptoms of depression go down.

9. OUR RELATIONSHIPS WITH OTHER PEOPLE IMPROVE.

Why wouldn't our relationships with other people improve? After we have begun to put into place our daily program for recovery, through prayer and meditation we now are expectant and hopeful. We reflect upon each step, and we complete a piece of the structure that in time will be the new me. I think that one of the more critical areas to mend in our lives is the thinking part of our selves. Depression appears to start with the way our minds react to and perceive events outside of ourselves. So, from the start we need to promote to those persons depressed to get involved in as much physical activity as possible, viz., walk, express personal feelings to others, go to meetings, talk on the phone with supportive people, in other words, get connected as much as possible. Most importantly we discover at our group meetings that there are many persons, much like ourselves and at the same level of recovery. We know we are not alone.

One of the immutable truths, according to Dorothy Rowe, who wrote the award winning book, Depression: The Way out of your Prison is "that other people are such that I must fear, envy or hate them." If we believe that we are bad and valueless then it follows that we must fear other people because they can find out how bad we are and so reject us.

Once newcomers hear the before and after of our lives it will make it easier for them to believe us when they experience our own enthusiasm and cheerfulness. (3)

We also believe that what you think is what you become. We can learn something not only about alcoholism but depression as well when Bill W., stated, that he can settle for mediocrity and self-satisfaction even though this may indeed prove to be a precarious perch. Or he (she) can choose to go on growing in greatness of spirit and action.

One of the best ways to grow out of our addictions is to start acting the healer instead of being the passive victim. We are under the care of no one except our God. (3)

I believe that our involvement with people like ourselves in the group can gradually broaden our perspective in the area of hope. We learn to utilize new found tools that help us live with hope as well as enable us to learn that we have to be active in our own recovery. In retrospect, we know that it is in our making amends to those we have harmed by our depression that opens our lives to those around us. Even if those to whom we make amends don't accept our amends the main thing is that we have made them. We are doing the amends for ourselves. Whether or not the other accepts our amends is none of our business and is out of our control

10. FEAR OF PEOPLE AND ECONOMIC INSECURITY WILL LEAVE US.

Losses may produce a variety of very intense and painful feelings. Fear can cripple the best of us. Why fear people and economic insecurity? In Steps 4, 5, 6, 7, 8, 9 we have examined our lives piece by piece, ending up with a good conscience, while feeling neither guilt nor shame for things of our past. We have thrown off the shackles of the past.

Bill, in his personal testimony in the DA book relates that you don't get better overnight, but you do get much better. I was down in the muck as far as I could go. I had to go and open the door for the first time because there was no other place to go. I had already used up all the hiding places in my life. I still have many problems like anyone else, but when I need sleep very badly, I turn this problem over to the Higher Power and go to sleep. I can always pick life up the next morning. Somehow it all gets done. Every few days the world dumps on you and beats you down. That's just life... (3)

I believe this man definitely "got it" when he began attending the group, spending some quiet time every day and learning that people like himself were able together to form a new environment, a surrogate family if you will, where there exists healing and hope.

Granted the group cannot find you a job or take away fear of people, but it can provide you with a map where you can discover a way out of the prison of one's depression. How do you learn that?

Kim, a member of DA in her personal story says that the moment that I read that I had a <u>choice</u> to stay in depression I undoubtedly knew that I could make the <u>choice</u> to get out of my depression. Bingo! It wasn't an illness. This did not have control over me. And another tool I use frequently through the DA manual is that "thoughts produce feelings, feelings produce moods and moods produce behavior. (3)

In the tradition of one major religion, there exist the three poisons, greed, anger and delusion. And as the saying goes "You can let your thoughts come into your mind. Just don't invite them to stay for tea."

In the Bible it states

"Fear not, for I am with you. Let not your heart be troubled."

11. INTUITIVELY KNOW HOW TO HANDLE SITUATIONS WHICH USED TO BAFFLE US.

As my mind began to heal and my thoughts became more lucid it became apparent that something inside me is changing. Depression, when you begin to examine the various symptoms up close, and deal with them, the experience becomes less threatening. Some say that depression is a collection of behaviors that are brought into play to defend us against things that are too painful to face. Also, depression results when a love object is lost through death or that one feels abandoned. We have become so at one with our lost love, that we mourn the death of part of us. The love object and ourselves has become one. I believe we use the word co-dependence today.

At first I was frightened by my various symptoms of depression. The symptoms proved to be baffling. I was not able to get out of bed as well as being unable to concentrate or manage a complex thought. I began to worry that I was losing my mind and I often asked myself if I was going to survive. But now my ability to handle situations in a meaningful way is due to my frequent attendance at meetings, and by making a daily time for prayer and meditation and a feeling that my life has purpose and meaning. The more I am physically active, i.e., going to meetings even when I don't feel like it. Working in my Depressed Anonymous Workbook, reading my 12-step literature.

This behavior is where my freedom begins. And yes, I do feel lousy at times but I also know that nothing can stand in my way to make <u>choices</u> in my own behalf. Previous to my involvement with the group I had no idea that my depression was not so powerful as to prevent me from even thinking that I could choose to feel differently.

The group meeting is where trust and openness is promoted among the fellowship. My defenses gradually lessen at every meeting and now I find my self-speaking about myself. I now believe that with my new openness no one will discredit or abandon me. I now feel secure in this new fellowship of persons who are just like me. I can live in hope and not despair. I learn that trust leads to freedom.

In the personal testimony portion of the Depressed Anonymous Manual, a Depressed Anonymous member, Starr shares how the group meeting gives a feeling of empowerment to those who want to share their story as a person that has suffered depression since childhood I can say that <u>until you start to open up</u>, share your hurts and feelings, listen to members of the group, watching them as they grow from the support of the group, you will not be able to get out of the prison of your depression. (3)

12. WE WOULD SUDDENLY REALIZE THAT GOD IS DOING FOR US WHAT WE COULD NOT DO FOR OURSELVES.

This I believe is at the core of our recovery and restoration... It is precisely at this moment in our lives that we realize that somebody, someone greater than myself is guiding me. This someone is not forcing us but is guiding us through our darkness. It is lighting our path so we neither stumble nor regress into our old ways of thinking and behaving. It is with this in mind that we continually redirect our attention to have that desire to do its will.

Before we discovered the program of Depressed Anonymous we were convinced that the only chance that we had to get better was to wait while the drugs kicked in and then everything would be all right. But now we are certain that our ability to get well is based on how much we develop the belief that we can choose how we feel and think. Indeed, we are now convinced that we can either sad ourselves or choose not to sad ourselves. The community and common bonds of the Depressed Anonymous fellowship produce a feeling that as other members of the group are recovering, so can I.

We must be willing to let go of all thoughts that tell us that we will never get well. These are the same thoughts that have imprisoned us over the years. We now listen to the god of our understanding and proceed with the belief that what we hold about the world on the outside of us is determined and governed by the world that is lived within us.

We are in a brand new way, on a new path, and find ourselves committed to a fresh belief that something powerful is starting to blossom within me. A peace that surpasses all understanding is beginning to be born as we learn to relax and wait and listen for that still small voice. We let go, we surrender, and we relax and let it speak. We pray that the God of our understanding make a way out of this desert of misery just as it has already created a way for those of us who live in the fellowship. Our thoughts move inside us with light and peace.

13. THESE PROMISES WILL ALWAYS ATERIALIZE IF WE WORK FOR THEM.

And how do we work for them so that they will materialize? First we read our Depressed Anonymous Manual, and apply what we have read in each Step and utilize the Depressed Anonymous Workbook. And of course we go to as many meetings as is possible and apply the 12 Step spiritual principles of recovery to our daily life. Also get a sponsor, which is a person who is familiar with the Steps and who applies these spiritual principles in their own life. The sponsor and you will meet as often as agreed and he/she will help guide you along the road to recovery. In time and with work you will feel the release and freedom provided by having had a "true spiritual awakening" which can keep you in God's will. This happens to be God's plan, so, always remember to stick to the plan. Good things begin to happen to us when we live in God's will. And that's a PROMISE!

CHAPTER SIX

COMPULSIONS AND CHOICES: THE ADDICTIVE NATURE OF THE DEPRESSION EXPERIENCE.

"It's our addictive thinking, our compulsive way of processing negative information, which means that we habitually store the negative and dump the positive influx of information and that gets us wanting to fall back in the old habit of staying isolated and avoiding others. We might fool ourselves and say that people have nothing to offer me so that I distance myself from everyone. Part of my nature when depressed is to avoid and distance myself from whatever I feel is threatening, like a child afraid of the dark. (10)

Freud theorized that the reason a person continues to do the circular dance within themselves is an effort to touch an unpleasant early life behavior or event long since buried in one's unconscious The circular dance, which promotes our addictive nature and the compulsion to repeat is an effort by our mind to somehow touch the unconscious in an effort to remember what it was that is the cause of our present cycle of misery, spinning around and round – looking for answers to why we do what we do and feel the way that we do, but never able to unlock the prison of our sadness.

It is my belief, after participating in hundreds of DA meetings over these past 25 years that this compulsion to repeat these self-destructive thoughts and images can be broken by attendance at our

I'LL DO IT WHEN I FEEL BETTER

group meetings. It is at the meetings where these unpleasant feelings, swallowed these many years can eventually be brought safely out into the light and accepted by the fellowship. No one puts me down for saying I am depressed. We never hear a "snap out of it" at our meetings. If we could just snap out of it then there would not be a need for our group meetings.

So, the logjam of all these unpleasant feelings, all balled up into one, gradually gets untangled. The group fellowship accepts us for what and who we are. Gradually as we are able to tell our story — tell who we are and trust ourselves and our story with this group — we begin to feel again. We free ourselves of the deadness, which has not only isolated us but has kept us disconnected from family, friends and those who love us. As the Yiddish saying states "share you story – save your life." I have witnessed this miracle many, many times at our face-to-face Depressed Anonymous meetings. Now that I am learning how to choose a different way of thinking and feeling which can result in breaking up the cycle of my addictive thinking and behaving, I now lead a normal life where my depression addiction experiences, my seduction, are helping others get connected to those of us who are living in hope one day at a time.

The major task facing all of us is to make use of those remarkable tools for recovery that I have found in the fellowship of the Depressed Anonymous group. It is here that we have a real face-to-face community of people who know us by name, can call us anytime, anywhere, and whom we choose to mentor in the 12-step program of recovery. I now know and believe that I have a choice – to be depressed or not to be depressed.

FREEDOM TO CHOOSE OUR THOUGHTS

In 1890, William James roused himself from a prolonged depression with the realization that he had the infinitesimal but omnipotent freedom to choose between one thought and another. When this individual freedom is experienced as independent of any and all external circumstances, the specter of confinement, censure, neurotic anxiety, and death itself fades rapidly. (11)

So, as with any addiction to a substance, a relationship or habits of thought, the best way to deal with it is to admit that we have a problem and then begin to do something about it. The DA group, in my estimation is one of the ways for those who choose to walk our path, can attain such awesome results with our program of recovery that they "will be amazed before they are halfway through" just what is in store for them as they persevere in our program of recovery.

What we are learning here is that the Twelve Step program of recovery can be used to overcome any compulsive/ addictive behavior for that person who sincerely wants to get emotionally, physically and spiritually healthy. (3)

The ultimate resource, we contend, is oneself and one's desire to quit sadding themselves. It is just this simple – if we really believe in the concept of community – a community where people really care for each other – then our personal resources will begin to be utilized to their fullest. We will see how we are no longer alone in our battle with depression but we are now accepted for who we are and what we are. Depression has to be seen as a potentially life threatening reality or the work that we do on ourselves will be halfhearted. That is why we recommend that people attending DA for the first time keep coming back to least 6 to 10 meetings and don't just come to one meeting hoping that that is going to solve your problem. Remember, Depressed Anonymous is not a class – it is a mutual aid – helping experience where each of us brings to the fellowship what has worked for us in getting free of the bondage of depression. By sharing with our newfound friends in the fellowship we begin to live with hope and serenity.

Our ultimate resource is our willingness to believe that we will in time and with work get better. We can feel better too. You will finally come home to a group of people who have the same desire that you do, namely the desire to free oneself from the feeling of despair and hopelessness. But if my 20 years or more in the program mean anything –it is that I have been my own worst enemy. I now believe that I can become my own best resource for living a life free from fear, shame and anxiety. I am a believer that my ultimate resource is the God of my understanding. For some the Higher Power is the group. You know, "two heads are better than one." We also believe that the spiritual awakening that the program promotes is absolutely an essential feature of this program. I have finally trusted the God of my understanding that it will get me through each day, even minutes, hours at a time. I truly believe and know that I can choose the way I will feel! So will you. That's a promise. Come join us.

When we are depressed we ruminate and beat up on ourselves. We all know how this ruminating continues our spiraling downward into a deep isolation and sadness, with its concomitant inactivity.

Our compulsion is a circular form of cognitive abuse – we continue to beat ourselves up with every thought. In fact, we beat ourselves up so bad that gradually this self-hatred that plays itself out on the inside of our minds results in a tremendous amount of debilitating fatigue, isolation and mental confusion.

So it is my conviction that depression is very much an addiction to that spiraling process of thought, which once it gets rolling cannot be stopped and pushes us down into the dark pit of despair. But now, armed with my newly established consciousness of what results when we start out on this journey of destructive thoughts I now have the strength to stop the downward spiral as I become more conscious of where this destructive thinking is headed.

I now know those signs, red flags if you will which do warn me what lies ahead if I continue to think these self-defeating thoughts, relax my guard and begin isolating myself from activities that I know will bring life and a renewed purpose.

We now desire to share with you the reader the following selected quotes from the Depressed Anonymous "big Book" which are to help illustrate the addictive nature of depression and the cyclical nature of our compulsive thinking and behaving. Most of us need the fellowship of the group to keep ourselves honest and in recovery and our dark thoughts out in the open. (12)

I am investing in myself. I am making my recovery my highest priority. I may have been on all the antidepressant medications and I may have seen all the best counselors, psychiatrists and doctors, but now finally, I am going to a room full of depressed people who understand me. These people I discover are investing in themselves. What will I find there? I will find some of the most caring people on the face of the earth. Some of the group will have been coming for months. They say they are having more good days than bad and it's getting better. The more meetings they attend the better they feel and the more support they receive. They are feeling empowered. It's the miracle of the group. Instead of living with a compulsion to repeat old negative and life negating thoughts and feelings, we now have a compulsion to live with hope plus a desire for a brand new way of living. We are now about to change the way we live and not just the way we talk to ourselves. We are going to get a new life. (3)

The God as we understand God is what appeals to more and more persons as we admit our helplessness over our compulsive, depressive thinking, actions or behaviors. We feel we have lost all control over everything — including our very self! The depressed person is aware that one's unpleasant thinking is a cyclical and spiraling process where there is never a respite. This obsessive ness driven by one's feeling of guilt, shame and worthlessness is the fuel that continues our own isolation. This experience is not so much a psychopathology as it is a way for the human spirit to comfort itself. The depression then is more a disease of isolation and being disconnected than it is a biological disorder. (3)

In Depressed Anonymous it states that

> The overeater, gambler, smoker, sexual addict are all driven by their compulsions. The emptiness of our lives is like a hole that continuously needs to be filled with some compulsive and addictive behavior. By letting go of our excessive tightfisted hold on our life, which paradoxically it causes us to lose hold; we start to face reality for the first time without the crippling crutch of our compulsion. We let go of our compulsion to repeat--the ritual of addictions. (3)

> ...Gradually over time, and due to being able to say no to the impulse to smoke, you feel stronger and so the painful withdrawal becomes less intense. The same applies to the addiction of depression in that at first it's difficult to stop completely the compulsive repeating of sad thoughts, but with time and working our Twelve Steps, and by our active involvement with DA we have the strength to say no to these sad thoughts and begin to choose hope and serenity instead. (3)

Instinctively, pain of any type tells us that if we have a problem it is imperative that we begin to do something about it. The Depressed Anonymous group, in my estimation, is one of the better ways for those who choose to help themselves while simultaneously helping others.

We know we only have today to live our life and we want to live with hope today because today is all we have – yesterday is gone forever and tomorrow isn't here yet. These Twelve Steps work for those who work the program and who try to live one day at a time. Many times we have been so scared of being rejected once more that we have withdrawn deeper into the anguish of our shame and hurt. We need to air our hurts, our shame, and let others hear our story. There is something healing about hearing ourselves speak to others about our own journey in life and the many emotional potholes that we have fallen into from time to time. We have felt our lives were jinxed! But now we can begin to feel hopeful when other members of the group shake their heads in knowing approval of what we are saying when we tell our story. Most have been where we are now. And the more we make an effort to come to meetings regularly, the more we will find members of the group telling us how they are seeing a change in the way we act, talk and look. We will accept the group's comments as being true and honestly expressed. These people speak our language and they all have been where we are now. You gradually begin to see yourself as healer instead of victim the more you work the program and get excited about the possibilities of helping others. When you start reaching out to others in the group it is at that point that you are carrying the message of hope to others. You have a future with Depressed Anonymous

We all know that any addictive/ compulsive type of behavior gradually removes you from the regular activities of persons around you, including family friends and coworkers, until you are established in the narrow confines of pain and isolation. We are always going to be just a little more isolated the more we try to think our addiction through in the circle of our own thoughts.

This is what I have found out about addictions/compulsions is that they are like that of a dog chasing his tail. It's a circular dance that can never end. The dog can never catch his tail. The addict can never get enough of what they are chasing, be it one substance or the other. The next physical rush is the next hit, the next drink, the next porno movie/picture.

Once we have admitted that our lives are powerless and unmanageable we begin to get excited about a vision, a vision of the new person that we might become. We also learn that there are other alternative ways and various choices that we can make in our behalf. It is beginning to sink into our minds that we are truly responsible for our choices and personal decisions. Like others in the program of recovery who broke out of the vise grip of their addictions they slowly learned to make decisions that favored sobriety and serenity.

Of the many discussions that center on the subject of depression, there appears to be a paucity of references to depression and its relationship to society.

"No man is an island," says the poet John Dunne. We live in a society where we find ourselves saturated with every form of electronic communication systems and are able to communicate with anyone, anywhere in the world. In a certain paradoxical way we at the same time appear to be moving toward greater isolation and human disconnection. The paradox of our times is that the more we are able to communicate with each other, it seems the more isolated we have become from each other. The number of people depressed is of epidemic proportions and how can this be, we may ask. There are now so many of us who are connected via the Internet, email, and social online groups as well as other sophisticated forms of communications.

This brings me to the point of this essay, namely, that if our world needs anything, it needs a world where people can get connected, network, form real communities where people know us and truly care about us. We all want a real live community –a face-to-face community where we can share, we can cry and we can laugh and where we can actually touch each other. Even though these modern ways of communicating are tremendous helps in moving past our isolation and into the real world they cannot end there.

A prisoner once mentioned how he considered depression not as a chemical imbalance but rather more of a living imbalance.

I personally can relate to that.

Our willingness to hand over to other people and organizations the responsibility which is ours (just as the color of our eyes is ours) stems from our inchoate desire to sink into the mindless bliss of being totally cared for, totally supported, our original wanting and getting everything. We do not want to accept that just as our eyes are organized to see only part of the spectrum of light and no others, so our sense of time is ordered to perceive time only as progressing, never as standing still or going backwards. No matter how great our longing, we cannot return to the womb of the Garden of Eden. (13)

We believe that with trust comes hope. We would like to stimulate you to get another picture of who you are and what you want to become. I think in our formative years our parents, guardians sometimes gave us mixed messages as to who we were. The many times we found that when someone said we would never amount to anything – we usually believed that they must be right and the prophecy became real as we got older. What we want to accomplish here is to promote a belief in you that you can change the way you think about yourself by the way you begin to picture yourself. So many times we get the picture that believing is truly seeing. We then begin in time to learn that even though we have a problem of depression and we thought there was no solution we gradually discovered through the 12 steps that yes we have a problem, but yes we also have found a solution and that solution is practical, concrete and one that will lead us gradually out of the prison of depression. What we must do to get to this healing and turning point is to have the desire to take responsibility for our thoughts, feelings and behaviors. Our 12 Step program of recovery with all its spiritual principles for right behavior will definitely direct us to the point where we need to be. It is here that we will find serenity and purpose for our lives.

CHAPTER SEVEN

HOPE
"Hope is a hard habit to break."
Brad Cohen in Front of the Class

The following instruction, HOW DEPRESSED ANONYMOUS WORKS is read at every Depressed Anonymous meeting.

You are about to witness the miracle of the group. You are joining a group of people who are on a journey of hope and who mutually care for each other. You will hear how hope, light and energy have been regained by those who were hopeless and in a black hole and tired of living.

By our involvement in the group we are feeling that there is hope--there is a chance for me too--I can get better. But we are not the people with the magic pills and the easy formula for success. We believe that to get out of the prison of depression takes time and work. (3)

And so at each and every Depressed Anonymous meeting the group listens as we hear what it will take to escape from the prison of depression.

Also at every meeting of the fellowship we hear how by using the spiritual tools, our Twelve Steps, we can gradually find the path that will and can lead us out into the light of freedom. We come to believe that a power greater than ourselves can restore us to sanity. And then we make a decision to turn our lives and our wills over to the God as we understand God.

To paraphrase Linda, who shares her personal story in the Depressed Anonymous "Big Book" she states that:

DA has pointed to the only hope there is- namely a Higher Power. A belief in something bigger than ourselves. Call it what you will, this Higher Power is the key, the life and the hope... (3)

The following quotes which speak to us about hope are those spoken to us in the writings of Depressed Anonymous members.

Ray says that:

The most important power in Depressed Anonymous is hope. We hope that we will not be locked in the prison of depression forever and that there is a way out for each one of us. A hope that our Higher Power will work the miracle through us and that we will find our own happiness. I have hope that our hearts and minds will know love and peace like we have never known or felt before. The power of Depressed Anonymous works for me. I hope and pray that it works for you. Keep coming back. (3)

A PATH OF HOPE

Ray continues to talk about the various parts that make up one's progress on the path to recovery:
I think most depression sufferer's go through a time of hopelessness and this feeling is very disabling for many of us. But with most problems or illnesses there is always hope. Hope that our problem will be solved or that we will get better. So if hope is part of the solution, how do we find our own path of hope?

Before we take that path I think it is important to see how the path is formed.

1. The first item is choices. We make choices every day for ourselves, some simple, and some complex. These choices may affect us for the rest of our lives, that is, what do I want to do in life? What do I want from life? What are my goals in life? Our lives are formed and maybe our own meaning of what life is, is revealed to us. So our path is first formed with the choices that that we make.

2. Next comes acceptance. Acceptance for who and what we are, accepting our own ideas, values, feelings, and emotions but even more important is accepting the fact that we can change our ideas, values, feelings and emotions. Accepting the fact that those changes can and will be made by ourselves and other people can't do that for us. They can only add to or detract from those changes. By accepting our choices and taking responsibility for those choices for our journey on the path of hope has begun.

3. The third item is trust. Trust in ourselves to make the right choices. Trust in ourselves to overcome any obstacle we face no matter how difficult it is. Also trusting another person, especially when that person loves, cares or just believes in us. Trust is so important, it tells us we are not alone and we can accept and trust in another to help us down our chosen path as well as trusting in our self.

4. The last item is faith. Faith in ourselves that things will be solved even when no answer or solution is in sight or seems possible. Faith in others to help us when we need help and that they will be there for

us. Faith in God or our Higher Power and that thru him our anguish, our sorrow, our pain will be lifted. Faith in our path of hope.

The path of hope for depression sufferers is not easy to build or to find sometimes. That's why I think it is so important to take your medication, if medications are prescribed, see your Doctor, counselor or therapist and go to Depressed Anonymous meetings as often as you can. Remember – when all seems to be lost there is always hope. (7)

The quotes here following are taken verbatim from the Depressed Anonymous "Big Book" and they all speak to us of hope. You begin to live with more hope as you hear each member express their feelings on how their life was before DA and how it is now as they practice the Twelve Step program in their daily lives.

Depressed Anonymous means hope as long as you want to get out of the pit of depression and start to believe that little voice that whispers, 'Yes, I am hopeful, I will feel better too." The other members of Depressed Anonymous give me hope. Others have made it out of the lonely pit of depression and so can I… (3)

… We believe that honesty, openness and a willingness to quit depressing are the basic building blocks of our recovery. To admit our powerlessness and believe that there is a power greater than ourselves is what is going to give my life purpose and hope. And finally we believe that humility is the rock on which each of the Twelve Steps of DA is based. (3)

We can tell them we want to be different and that we are choosing a life filled with hope instead of a life filled with despair (3)

As you well know, when we say we are wrong we create an area of uncertainty ... if you cannot tolerate uncertainty then you cannot afford to admit that you are wrong. Absolute certainty may appear to you to be a wonderful thing, giving complete security, but have you ever considered that if you want absolute certainty you must give up freedom, love and hope. (3)

We now know that it is only when we actively involve ourselves in the first step of DA that we start the march toward recovery is what we seek as people depressed. We refuse to label ourselves as depressives because we do not intend to be depressed any longer than we have to. We are also more than our feelings of sadness. Our real identity is emerging from the sadness as we try to live one day at a time. (3)

Of course I am still testing it out but I feel better and for the first time in 14 years I have hope. It's not that hard to find something positive about myself or my life now. So, I remind myself of something positive every day and that's what I'm going to do until I don't have to remind myself anymore because I'll know. (3)

Remarkable things happen to us when we are willing to admit defeat and talk about our powerlessness over our depression and how our lives had become unmanageable. The first step is the beginning of the flight of steps that takes up and into our new way of living. At our fellowship of DA we talk hope, we act hopeful, and we think hope. We learn that our thinking depressed and negative thoughts might have got us in the shape that we are in today. What you think is what you become. For us who find sadness our second nature we at times continue to revert to the comfort of old familiar negative thinking and are in actuality returning to self-destructive activity. Sadness is overcome by hope. (3)

Empowerment and prevention are two realities that give us the push and the power for talking day after day with persons still suffering from depression. I know that some who hear about us will go with an expectant faith that they will find hope and peace in the group. This hope in itself may keep them from sliding down the slippery abyss of depression. Life is too short and the pain so devastating. Only by sharing my pain can I ever hope to reduce its size. (3)

Today I can experience hope. I will believe I can live this day with pleasant thoughts. I will do one activity that will give me hope and light for today." "...Today I will believe I can live this entire day "hopeful" and that I can return to the above activities anytime and as many times as I need to just for today (3)

...These people cannot afford the risk of living with hope. If everything is for certain then the reality of hope is superfluous. To live without certitude on a daily basis is to live with the unpredictability of life and so in a terrible form of logic they have conditioned themselves to see their personal world dark and gray without hope, i.e., lest it change. To live with change and the ramification of change means that I would have to take responsibility for my life, for my own feelings and the day to day adventure of living without certainty. (3)

If surrender of our wills to the "care of God" is of the essence of the spiritual life, for anyone who truly desires to free himself from self / herself from a chronic and compulsive behavior such as depression then the Twelve Steps can be your stepping stones to the path of a hope-filled life. (3)

Hope can exist only in a state of uncertainty. That certainly means total certainty. That certainty means to be without hope. The prison of depression is built with the bricks of total certainty.

"Certainty. Security. No hope."

To hope means to run the risk of disappointment. Avoid disappointment. Stay depressed. To be insecure means not to be in control. Stay in control. Be depressed. To be uncertain means to be unsure of the future. Predict the future with certainty. Stay depressed.

Hope can only exist when there is uncertainty. Absolute certainty means complete hopelessness. If we want to live fully we must have freedom, love and hope. So life must be an uncertain business. That is what makes life wholesome." (6)

In the matter of depression, Dr. Rowe warns us that when we predict that we will always be the way we are is to predict a life of certainty but one that is without hope. In the reality of the way we construct our world we begin to live with uncertainty and with the uncertainty we are going to little bit by little bit accept some pain. When we are depressed it is not so important to discover how we got to be depressed, but what is important is how we see our depression. Do we believe, like Dorothy Rowe, that we will always see ourselves as bad, worthless, unacceptable to ourselves and to others when we are depressed? If this is the way that we look at ourselves then we are sure to believe that we will never change. We hold these beliefs about ourselves as immutable truths-absolute and ever binding. This is the thing about depression-we believe that life will always be this way – possessed by hollow and deadly emptiness which we carry around in our bodies, day after day, year after year.

Our identity as persons depressed is to believe that we are always going to be the way we are now and be depressed forever. We know that it won't always have to be this way. Our identity is that of a free agent who has the option to choose misery for the rest of their lives or choose hope and live with some uncertainty that may bring us to a life filled with hope. The more we allow the feelings of pain and the unpleasantness of our feelings to surface the more we will live in uncertainty and hope. To live with uncertainty is to live with some hope that our tomorrow will be different than today. We hope for things not yet seen. We hope for things to be different. This is the identity of a person who is working the Twelve Steps of Depressed Anonymous. (15)

CHAPTER EIGHT

TRUST

"When you're depressed all you're interested in is survival."
 Dorothy Rowe.

In this chapter I would like to acquaint you with an assortment of thoughts excerpted mainly from the Depressed Anonymous book and from the writings of Dr. Dorothy Rowe, Ph.D. These thoughts deal with the issue of trust. Trust, always has been a critical element in one's search for finding one's true and best self. And with trust comes hope. Hope is the thread which weaves its way throughout the spiritual program of the Twelve Steps.

I remember Fred on his first visit to DA. He said that he had been depressed all his life. The group listened to Fred, and of course for the most part Fred said he didn't have the foggiest notion what all this talk of God had to do with his sadness and how it was supposed to help him. [Step 3] But it was the pain of Fred's depression that brought him back time after time to the meetings, and he started not only to feel better but he began to look better. Then as he heard more about the Twelve Steps he saw that he could trust this Higher Power. And that maybe the depression that had been such a lifetime companion was not for him anymore. Fred took the plunge, came to believe that a power greater than himself could restore him to sanity – and it did just that. Fred said he didn't need this depression anymore got busy making amends to family, friends and co-workers for being such a negative person, and began to take inventory where he needed to spring clean his house. (3)

It appears that Fred is like many of those who come to attend their first Depressed Anonymous meeting. They come fearing that the risk that they are taking by attending a depressed meeting, like everything they have tried, will not produce any positive results. They figure that no one could possibly love them for themselves.

THE GOD OF OUR UNDERSTANDING

We learn that there is a God who is supposed to love us and take care of us, but we are afraid to let go of who we believe we are or what we feel we have to be. Trust is something that we have given up a long time ago. Trust is hard for us, especially when we feel that life, people and our circumstances have completely let us down. For so long now unpleasant feelings have led us to believe that we have no right to happiness, now or in the future. We have grown up with a sense of suspicion of those around us who appear happy and satisfied with life. Instead we find it safer to back away from too much involvement with other people, because they would see how bad we really are if they got to know us and then our secret would be out. We don't ever know what "normal" feels like, because we constantly feel so hollow and empty inside. (3)

...Recovery is being able to trust ourselves in exploring ways to feel our emotions (3)

There needs to be openness, willingness and honesty if we are to find the truth about ourselves.

And in the case of our friend Fred we find that he first admitted he had a problem when he walked into the Depressed Anonymous meeting. He knew that he needed help. And after listening to the other members of the fellowship he realized that it was because of believing in something bigger than himself (initially the group) that was the change that began to turn him around. And after a number of weekly meetings Fred began to make sense out of his own life experiences by hearing the stories of the members who like him were gradually climbing out of that dark pit of life called depression. And it was at this point that Fred felt he could trust his story of pain and hurt with those in the fellowship with whom he now could relate. He felt he was home. Fred now had the tools and the key that allowed him to travel on the road to freedom and serenity.

The essence of the experience of depression is that you are alone in some kind of prison.... When we are simply unhappy, no matter what terrible fate has befallen us, we still possess a connection to the rest of the world and to ourselves. We let others comfort us, and feel warmed and supported, and we comfort ourselves. But when we are depressed, no warmth or support comes through our prison wall, and we punish ourselves most cruelly. (14)

We have to give Fred and all those like him credit for taking the risk to go to their first meeting with hope that they might find help there. And at the first meeting every newcomer has the chance to grab onto the key – the key that will open the doors to the light of day for each and every day of their lives. They can receive the key that unlocks the door to their prison.

And when they begin to walk on this new found road to freedom they will share this freedom key with all the other fellow travelers whom they meet on the path. Fred's trust is not only paying off for Fred but his trust is now paying off for others who have been locked up in the same prison of despair and aloneness.

Without the defense of depression the human race would not have survived. By shutting ourselves in this prison we keep out all the dangers and uncertainties that otherwise would overwhelm us. By making every day in the prison the same as the next, we deal only with the bare minimum of issues that we can manage to deal with, and we make sure that nothing new gets in to frighten and stress us. By concentrating on just ourselves we do not have to face what is happening to others. Locked in our prison we can avoid acknowledging that the inescapable disasters that the human race is prone to – death and loss and the tragedies that nature or our own cruelties and stupidities bring upon us. In depression we can give ourselves a breathing space before we confront all this again, or we can keep ourselves safely locked away forever. (14)

Depression is about lost selves--and the struggle to regain the self. We are in a perpetual lock down! It is indeed a battle with one's self to survive – that is why Dorothy Rowe calls depression a prison. We build the walls as a defense to keep us safe till we can combat our demons and find which way out is the best for us.

Over time you and I both have discovered a truth: trust is never an easy proposition. Trust comes with a belief that all things will work out. But another problem is that so much of our lives negative and harmful life experiences have been carried through life and so conditioned to predict that no matter what we say or do we will always be living in the prison of despair.

Eric Erickson knew that trust precedes hope and hope blossoms into a healthy autonomy. In his seven stages of human development he shows us how with trust grows originating from the very beginning of human development. He recognized that with trust leads to hope, with autonomy comes will, with initiative comes purpose, with Industry comes competence, with identity comes fidelity, with intimacy comes love, with generativity comes care, and with integrity comes wisdom.

And Dr. Rowe tells us that our experience can and does provide us with a respite of sorts:

She suggests that

Depression is the most popular of all the desperate defenses. The foundation of our prison of depression is our belief that, no matter how good I appear to be, I am bad, evil, unacceptable to myself and to other people. (14)

Dorothy Rowe once said that trusting oneself is an essential part of creativity. And why wouldn't trust of oneself be an essential part of creativity. We all recognize how spontaneity is the opposite of depression. The symptoms of depression not only paralyze us into inaction physically but likewise freeze our cognitive facilities so that not another thought can move forward so as to connect with another thought to form some meaningful sentence.

So to trust oneself can bring to one's life a new dimension of hope that there might be a possibility for a positive change. But we need to take the road less traveled – not the road that is worn and rutted with the traveled path of hopeless journeys and adventures. The road less traveled is the one that joins with fellow travelers who are filled with hope and purpose.

Rowe says that by listening to our inner voice and so trusting that quiet inner voice is the beginning of getting help for your self and serves as the key out of depression. Bill W., says that as time passes and we begin to "get" the program of recovery that we are better suited now to follow those intuitive hunches which come with our renewed trust in self and the god of our understanding.

...Now I am deciding to think, act and behave differently, much to my personal credit and a new found trust in a Higher Power. I am a sailor who sees the land, knows the right direction and does the rowing to get where I want to go. The twelve Steps are my compasses. I also know that this group of people, which we call DA, will help me assume a sense of no longer feeling out of control. Instead I believe I will begin to take responsibility for my life and risk getting better. In time I can trust the group with my story and my struggles against the heaviness of daily life. In time I can trust God to take away my hurts and pains and sadness, just as I have begun to trust the members of DA with my deepest hurts and feelings of loneliness (3)

Trust and risk seem to be two sides of the same coin that we know as life. And as it says in DEPRESSED ANONYMOUS, I need to take responsibility for my life, thoughts and behaviors.

We learn from Fred and the thousands of others who willingly risk leaving their comfort zone and begin traveling into the land of the unknown.

Dorothy Rowe in the Foreword to Depressed Anonymous speaks about our Twelve Step program of recovery making the statement

...Most of all, it (DA Manual) shows how we can discover the essential unity of loving and accepting ourselves and one another, of being close to others, and experiencing the sense of oneness in all in which we can reside in acceptance and trust. (3)

We all know and have experienced the truth that by trusting others with our deepest hurts and fears this sometimes can reduce the size of these very same obstacles to happiness. We might also have felt God's presence for the first time as we began to experience a new sense of peace living inside of us.

When we look back, we realize that the things which came to us when we put ourselves in God's hands were better than anything we could have planned. (3)

And as a member of DA relates their experience in DEPRESSED ANONYMOUS; it gives us some hope that we are not alone in how we feel. Many of us as depressed persons find it hard to trust God. As equally bewildering is the idea of trusting ourselves. In working the Twelve Steps and attending DA MEETINGS I FOUND THAT I CAN TRUST God. Life is unpredictable and at times very difficult but this new understanding that we have of God and who loves me greatly wants to give us all the good that we can handle. Once I begin to trust God who loves me unconditionally then I might begin to love myself. (3)

And in another personal testimony

...I also began to trust God as my Higher Power. More and more I turned it over to the Higher Power and said I can't do these things all by myself. I did pray as hard as I could. I prayed every night. I believed that this change was going to happen. I started believing in me. But the wonderful thing was that I began to realize that I was no longer alone. A Higher Power was going to be there for me. (3)

I like what Dorothy Rowe says:

    This desire for perfect control of the environment and of oneself is based on profound mistrust of the controller. Because you see yourself as bad, you cannot trust yourself to be. Because you cannot trust yourself to become, to allow yourself to grow as a plant grows.

    And where does this mistrust originate? Many think that it goes back to the origins of our childhood experiences.

THE ORIGINS OF MISTRUST

Dr. Fitzgerald, a Psychiatrist, said the seedbed of mistrust resides in childhood. Many times this lack of trust, of others and self, and the world around them may have begun with the loss of a parent, brother, sister or close friend. Many times mistrust comes about because of an alcoholic parent so that a child never knows if the drunken loved one is coming home sober or in a drunken angry stupor. Anger and rejection by caregivers and or peers can also have an effect on the ability to trust. Parental divorce or separation can have an effect on the child.

Then during the developmental period of adolescence and because of poor body image and possible rejection by peers he/she is unable to trust him/herself or his confidence to play any part in his own development. It's pointed out that a lack of trust in the controller (the adult) and the ones who did not provide the basis for trust in early life now see how his/her thinking, emotions, behavior, health and spirituality have all been affected, to a greater or lesser extent even now in the adult life of the individual.

...Many times our lives have been traumatized from the very beginning of childhood when one or the other parent abandoned us, and we felt that loss deeply so that the sadness of a childhood never lived continues to motivate our every action. Our inability to live with any amount of trust makes it difficult to trust a Higher Power that it too won't abandon us or punish us like an early caretaker did when we were children. (3)

And how does one build character but by learning the tenets of one's own faith traditions or practices and trying to live them out in one's daily life. It is in the simple process of being willing, honest and open about the best paths to take in overcoming our negative life attachments that trust can be attained.

...Character is built by truth and the willingness to list the truth in ourselves. It can be a painful search but it will reveal that it's all right to be imperfect and not have all the answers not to be perfect. It's all right to trust others with our deepest fears and hurts, and to know that we can still be loved and respected even though we share how bad and evil we have considered ourselves over the years. It will be evident in time that one's feeling of deep sadness did not come out of nowhere but indeed was the result of the way we were led to believe and think about ourselves. (3)

I believe that I can honestly say that the co-founders of Alcoholics Anonymous say it best when they point out the basis for trust in ourselves comes about when our purpose and mission in this life begins to be realized. We are now on a different basis: the basis of trusting and relying upon God. We trust infinite God rather than our finite selves. Just to the extent that we do as we think He would have us do, and honestly rely on him, does he enable us to match calamity with serenity. (4)

Every member of every 12 step fellowship is aware of the power of the following prayer, which in itself has been found to produce and promote the growth of trust in the lives of those who pray this prayer.

God grant me the serenity to accept the things I cannot change, the courage to change the things I can, and the wisdom to know the difference.

CHAPTER NINE

SPIRITUALITY AND DEPRESSION

We make no apologies for our faith in a God that can restore one to sanity but to serenity and joy as well. "We never apologize for God. Instead, we let God demonstrate, through us, what God can do. We ask God to remove our fear and direct our attention to what God would have us be. At once, we commence to outgrow fear (4)

A 16th century physician said this about melancholia Fear and sorrow are the true characters and inseparable companions of most melancholy, not all. (16)

We claim spiritual progress rather than spiritual perfection. (4)

Paracelsus (1493-1541) a medieval physician, mystic and alchemist are of the opinion that such spiritual diseases (melancholia), are spiritually to be cured... Ordinary means in such cases will not avail; we must not struggle with god, physicians and physic can do no good, we must submit ourselves unto the mighty hand of God, acknowledge our offences, call to him for mercy ... He alone must help: otherwise our diseases are incurable, and we not are relieved. (16)

In his voluminous work THE ANATOMY OF MELANCHOLIA first published in 1621 the author traces the historical understating of melancholia or depression as we know it today. Already back in the 16th century this alchemist Paracelsus and physician rightly spoke about depression being a disease of the spirit and that a spiritual solution need be sought for relief.

Paracelsus held the conviction that God has to be part of the healing as melancholia for him was a spiritual disease and so needed a spiritual cure. And now the insight and belief put forward by Paracelsus in the present time is being echoed in our own time by Bill W., and all those who are availing themselves of the spirituality of the Twelve Steps. All members of Twelve Step fellowships who are acknowledging the importance of a belief in a power greater than themselves have the guiding star of hope and meaning in their daily lives.

Research from the National Institute for Healthcare Research

A recent study in the American Journal of Psychiatry identified this other often overlooked resource that patients draw upon to help fend off depression -a deep religious commitment – that significantly reduced recovery times. This study focused on 85 patients hospitalized with serious medical illnesses who also became depressed. Among their battery of tests, patients took the Hoge Intensive Religiosity Scale, which measures how deeply a person has internalized their religious values and faith.

Surprisingly, patients recovered from their depression 70 percent faster for every 10-point increase on the Hoge scale, which ranged from 10 to 50. This link held even when taking into account other factors that could speed up recovery including improving physical health. (NIFHR)

It has to be that what one believes is what one can become. Actually it is a self-fulfilling prophecy that how we conceive of our self is what we can become. This having a dream and setting out some life goals can lead to a life filled with hope and promises. And for those of us who take our 12-step fellowship seriously and stay actively involved one day at a time soon discover the joy and serenity that this spiritually rich recovery program provides.

I would like to share with you some salient points made by people coming from different points of view regarding the essential reality that we call spirituality. We all know the difference between spirituality and religion. And as you reflect upon this difference you can better understand the principles of 12 step spirituality.

In the paragraph following, Bob P, a charter member of Depressed Anonymous shares his thoughts on the subject of SPIRITUALITY AND DEPRESSION.

Spirituality involves the recognition and acceptance of a Higher Power beyond your own will and intelligence, with whom you can have a relationship. This Higher Power can provide you with an experience of joy, security, peace of mind, and guidance that goes beyond what is possible in the absence of the conviction that such a power exists. Spirituality can be seen as being distinct from religion. Different world religions have proposed various doctrines and belief systems about the nature of a Higher Power and humanity's relationship to it. Spirituality, on the other hand, refers to the common experience behind these various points of view – an experience involving the awareness of a relationship with something that transcends your personal self as well as the humane order of things.

The "something" has been given various names---"God" being the most popular in Western society – and is defined in ways that are too numerous to count. Here it will be referred to simply as the Higher Power. You can choose to define what that means for yourself in whatever way feels most appropriate to you. Your own sense of Higher Power can be as abstract as cosmic consciousness: or as down to earth as the beauty of the oceans and the mountains. Even if you consider yourself a non-believer, you may get a sense of inspiration from taking a walk in the forest or contemplating a beautiful sunset. Or a small child's smile may give you a special sense of joy. Whatever inspires you and takes you beyond yourself into a larger perspective is the direction of what is referred here as your Higher Power. (7)

In the following quotation Bill W., gives us his concept of God. By doing so he has basically reframed all of our understanding of God.

When, therefore, we speak to you of God, we mean your own conception of God. This applies, too, to others spiritual expressions, which you find in this book. Do not let any prejudices you may have against spiritual terms deter you from honestly asking yourself what they mean to you? At the start, this was all we needed to commence spiritual growth, to affect our first conscious relation with God, as we understand him. Afterward, we found ourselves accepting many things, which often seemed entirely out of reach. That was growth, but if we wished to grow we had to begin somewhere. So we used our own conception, however limited it was.

We need to ask ourselves but one short question. Do I now believe, or am I even willing to believe, that there is a power greater than myself? As soon as a person can say that he or she does believe or is willing to believe, we emphatically assure him or her that they are on their way. It has been repeatedly proven among us that this simple cornerstone a wonderfully effective spiritual structure can be built. (4)

In the Twelve and Twelve, in the discussion on Step Two the author states you can, if you wish, make AA itself your 'higher power.' Here's a very large group of people who have solved the alcohol problem. In this respect they are certainly a power greater than you, who have not even come close to a solution. Surely you can have faith in them. Even the minimum of faith will be enough. You will find many members who have crossed the threshold just this way. All of them will tell you, once across, their faith broadened and deepened. Relieved of the alcohol obsession, their lives unaccountably transformed they came to believe in a Higher Power, and most of them began to talk of God. (18)

CURE AND CARE

Dr. David Karp, a Sociologist from Boston University in his work speaking of Sadness wrote the following insights about depression

... (I) commented that once individuals realize that medical treatment is unlikely to fix their problem, their thinking moves away from the medical language of cure and toward the spiritual language of transformation. With that interpretation I was speaking only as a sociologist trying to see patterns in data. Several weeks later I read a nearly identical idea in Moiré's book. (Care of the Soul, Thomas Moore). Moore, a theologian and philosopher writes, "A major difference between care and cure is that cure implies the end of trouble.... But care has a sense of ongoing attention. There is no end. Conflicts may never be resolved. Your character will never change radically, although it may go through some interesting transformation. Awareness can change, of course, but problems persist and never go suffering and do not offer the illusion of a problem-free-life."

---- Moore sustains the argument that we ought not pathologize depression. He makes the interesting point that the word "depression" itself shapes the way we think about the human condition it describes. Today, consistent with a medically dominated view of emotional pain, we prefer the more clinical and serious word depression to the more human words "melancholy" or "sadness." This observation is entirely consistent with labeling theory in social psychology that ties the construction of our identities to the labels others apply to us and that we ourselves ultimately adopt. (1)

One of the major indicators of depression is how it permeates our soul with that desire for isolation and being disconnected from life around us. In fact the opposite of depression is not happiness, but instead it is lack of spontaneity and feeling alive and living with meaning. The various symptoms of depression can cause our thoughts to slow, our mind becomes paralyzed and most of our desires to participate in life come to a standstill. Physically we shut down.

A depressed person gains by getting in touch with a Higher Power, something or someone larger than oneself. For many of us it is the God of our understanding as worshiped in a community of believers.

I think it was interesting to read Bill W's., spiritual experience when he finally met the "God of the preachers" as he lay sick in the hospital and witnessed the hospital room being lit up with that very presence of God. This was the spiritual experience that we must have, not necessarily just like Bill's but nevertheless an experience of meeting God and surrendering to God's will for our life. This experience of finally saying our "yes" to God's will simultaneously speaks the necessary "no" to whatever attachment had us by the throat and into the self-destruction mode.

Having had a spiritual awakening means that we are now aware that the core of our being is spiritual and is where our power resides. "The Kingdom of God is within you." This spiritual awakening occurred when we finally let the God of our understanding enter our lives and we surrendered our resistance to getting better. We soon discover that in our program that no compulsion can be controlled by will power alone – it must be surrendered to the Higher Power or to the care of the God of our understanding. It will in turn lift the burden from our backs. This is the spiritual awakening that keeps us from the sadness as we take the message of healing to others in the group who are new to the program. (3)

THAT VITAL SPIRITUAL EXPERIENCE
Meister Eckert (c.1260-1328)

"This work (birth), when it is perfect, will be due solely to God's action while you have been passive. If you really forsake your own knowledge and will, then surely and gladly God will enter with his knowledge shining clearly. Where God achieves self-consciousness, your own knowledge is of no use, nor has it standing. Do not imagine that your own intelligence may rise to it, so that you may know God. Indeed, when God divinely enlightens you, no natural light is required to bring that about. This (natural light) must in fact be completely extinguished before God will shine in with his light, bringing back with God all that you have forsaken and a thousand times more, together with a new form to contain it all. (3)

PRAYER AND MEDITATION AND ITS REWARDS

Perhaps one of the greatest rewards of meditation and prayer is the sense of belonging that comes to us. We no longer live in a completely hostile world. We are no longer lost and frightened and purposeless. The moment we catch

even a glimpse of God's will, the moment we begin to see truth, justice, and love as the real and eternal things in life. We are no longer deeply disturbed by all the seeming evidence to the contrary that surrounds us in purely human affairs. We know that God lovingly watches over us. We know that when we turn to him, all will be well with us, here and hereafter. (18)

For his audience, the alcoholic, Bill W., gives them a respite from having to think of God in terms of tyrant, taskmaster, or disciplinarian. Instead he allows us to believe in a God of our own understanding. This God can be our Higher Power, or that force for good which will give us the chance, again, to redirect our energies to that which will free us so as to live with sanity, sobriety and that new fellowship of like-minded seekers. Fortified with this concept of God, we have been given the freedom to see God in a new light.

I KNOW I AM NO LONGER ALONE!

This is a very important passage for us because of the Newcomers who attend our group for the first time (who by the way enable us to see ourselves) and who are told that they never have to speak, never have to give their names and they can pass without speaking while each member of the group has their opportunity to speak. But it has been my experience that those who do come for the first time and who listen to one speaker after the next find that truly this group speaks their language, a language of hope. They are no longer alone. They feel that they are home. Being connected to something bigger than ourselves is a great beginning for every one of us. I believe that because we are social beings and are part of a community beginning at birth with a Father and a Mother that this small nucleus of a community added to all the other members of this extended community it is here where we learn about the world, and our relationship to it. Will we be in awe of it or will we be frightened by it.

And for many of us, beginning at a tender age, are introduced to the God of our family. We are connected to a Higher Power. We are connected to all our brothers and sisters here and everywhere. We are all cousins!

...I maintain that the social disconnection generated by an ethic of individualism is an important element in the proliferation of affective disorders in America. Assuming that position is correct, what can we do about it concretely ... (1)

STEP TWO AND STEP THREE OF DEPRESSED ANONYMOUS

(Step 2) Came to believe that a power greater than myself could restore me to sanity.

(Step 3) Made a decision to turn my life and my will over to the care of God as I understand God.

These steps stress the importance of a someone, a something that is bigger than ourselves, bigger than our depression, bigger than our compulsive need to bash ourselves with self-deprecating thoughts. We are in need of some power that truly restores us to sanity. We can be restored!

As soon as we admitted the possible existence of a Creative intelligence, a Spirit of the Universe underlying the totality of things, we began to be possessed of a new sense of power and direction, provided we took other simple steps. We found that God does not make too hard terms with those who seek him. To us, the Realm of the Spirit is broad, roomy, all inclusive; never exclusive or forbidding to those who earnestly seek. It is open; we believe to all men ... We needed to ask ourselves but one short question. "Do I now believe or am I even willing to believe, that there is a Power greater than myself?" As soon as a man can say that he does believe or is willing to believe, we emphatically assure him that he is on his way. It has been repeatedly proven among us that upon this simple cornerstone a wonderfully effective spiritual structure can be built. (4)

You are asking yourself, as all of us must: "Who am I? Where am I?" ..."Whence do I go?" The process of enlightenment is usually slow. But, in the end, our seeking always brings a finding. These great mysteries are, after all, enshrined in complete simplicity.

The willingness to grow is the essence of all spiritual development. (2)

MODERN LIFE AND DEPRESSION

The medical Psychiatrist Dr. Dominique Meggle points out in his talk at an International symposium on Depression in Rome that modern man, who is individualistic, is enough for himself. He boasts of being a nomad. He does not admit that changes can modify him. He does not have exchanges; he has experiences that are sufficient for him to continue-at the same level-sex, food, or music. Upholding his freedom and sincerity of his feelings, he has replaced being with having. He consumes and after gaining enjoyment, he feels sad. Pornography spreads in all directions. It shows a form of sexuality to us that is nothing else but a consumer good. The modern form of this widespread depression has neither a biological nor a psychological cause. It is a form of depression that springs from something higher. It is a form of depression that comes from the removal of a meaning of existence: it is what Victor Frankel calls: noogenesis neurosis of existential depression." It belongs to the sphere of the mind and shows that a society that replaces being with having in a systematic way produces a whole series of depressed people. It makes them mad. The removal of meaning disturbs the human psyche and human cerebral biology.

In this case the good news takes two forms. On the one hand, we have the experimental proof that in order to function correctly the human being needs values and to be able to give meaning to his or her life. We can no longer deny the fact. It is in front of our very eyes. Given that we have done nearly everything that we should not have done, by exclusion we now know what we have to do to escape from the pandemic of man, his freedom, his values, his search for meaning but also his sense of responsibility, once again at the center and the summit of the whole of socials, economics and political life. (17a)

LETTING GO OF OUR COMPULSIONS

To conclude I must add some basic thoughts found in Depressed Anonymous at Appendix B, The Vital Spiritual Experience (3)

The Twelve Steps are the essential beliefs and at the very core of Depressed Anonymous. The DA recovery program, modeled on Alcoholics Anonymous which originally developed to help men and women deal with their addiction to alcohol, one day at a time. The Twelve Steps have been found to be a potent means of recovery for those who desire to free themselves from their compulsions. The twelve Steps are basically a program of letting go of our compulsions and handing over our will to the care of God, as we understand God. Essentially our program is a step-by-step way to change not only our addiction but also our way of life. Change happens when we choose to change. The fellowship of the group and our desiring to make change in our life is what provides our life-giving spiritual experience. Many people get organized religion and spirituality mixed up and DA achieves strength from spirituality without set creed, dogma or doctrine. All the program asks of a person who comes to the meetings is only to have a sincere desire to stop the compulsion of sadding themselves... (3)

It further states

The God as we understand God is what appeals to more and more persons as we admit our helplessness over our compulsive depressive thoughts, actions or behaviors. We feel we have lost all control over everything – including our thinking! The depressed person is aware that their unpleasant thinking is a cyclical and spiraling process where there is never a respite. This obsessiveness driven by one's feelings of guilt, shame and worthlessness is the fuel that continues our own isolation. This experience is not so much a psychopathology as it is a way for the human spirit to comfort itself. The depression then is more a disease of isolation and being disconnected than it is a biological disorder. The Twelve Step Program helps people to become God-conscious. It is in working the program, while making no excuses for the spiritual nature of our recovery. We can begin to attribute our newfound sense of hope and peace to the Higher Power. For the active member of Depressed Anonymous there begins to glimmer in the distance the bright light of hope. (3)

SERVICE GLADLY RENDERED

Service, gladly rendered, obligations squarely met, troubles well accepted or solved with God's help, the knowledge that at home or in the world outside we are partners in a common effort, the well understood fact that in God's sight all human beings are important, the proof that love freely given surely brings a full return, the certainty that we are no longer isolated and alone in a self-constructed prison, the surety that we no longer be square pegs in round holes but can fit and belong in God's scheme of things – these are the permanent and legitimate satisfactions of living for which no amount of pomp and circumstance, no heap of material possessions could possibly be substitutes.

True ambition is not what we thought it was. True ambition is the deep desire to live usefully and walk humbly under the grace of God. (18)

CHAPTER TEN

PRAYER AND MEDITATION

In AA (DA) we have found that the actual good results of prayer are beyond question. They are matters of knowledge and experience. All those who have persisted have found strength not normally their own. They have found wisdom beyond their usual capability. And they have increasingly found a peace of mind which can stand firm in the face of difficult circumstances. (2)

We need to develop a God-consciousness. (3)

A recovering alcoholic said:
In the Twelve Steps the word God is mentioned seven times, but the particular addiction – alcohol, drugs, gambling, etc. – is only mentioned once, in the first step. After a while you become so close to God, you really depend on God not just at prayer time but all day long. (3)

As we continue to mine the wealth of power that has been placed in our soul, we begin to realize that as we dig down with the hope of finding more direction from God for a life of serenity, the more there is to discover. This serenity is the paradox of goodness – the more you seek it, the more there is available for personal use and community sharing. The supply of God's guidance grows the more you make use of it. This means that the more we give into God's love and live in the Presence, the more time we have to be of service to those whom God puts in our path. Now we are more aware and conscious of our own needs. An inventory of our character defects and personal strengths help to develop our sensitivity to be the pulse of God's love in our hearts.

Meditation is a powerful force in "pausing" our lives. We "pause" our mind and that forward march which pushes us further away from ourselves. Now we can march to the still small voice which grows louder and louder the more we "pause" in our life and pray.

We now believe that it's God's will 1) To first of all be in touch with God on a continual and daily basis 2) that we stay connected with those much like ourselves, working a program based on spiritual principles. 3) That we be conscious of our own needs and those of others and 4) to remain in contact with all those who, like us, live with the powerful belief that with God all things are possible for us. As we continue to share with other members of the group we continue to grow in faith, humanness and service to each other.

It takes patience in these days of fast is good and faster is better. Today is the day of fast food and the drive thru. But as we learn over time, there seems to be no speedy way to gain spiritual maturity and freedom. And it is only with time, work and prayer that can deliver us from our character defects. If we desire that the Higher Power manifest its power in our life, then we soon learn that this God spirit must find its rest in our thoughts, mind and heart. I personally have felt these many times that the God of my understanding is especially active in the minds and hearts of those who share in the security and peace of the 12 step meeting.

We think about the 24 hours ahead when we wake up, and attempt to live the day in honesty and peace. We ask God to ward off thoughts of self-seeking, dishonesty and false motives. And as A.A., says, when we are faced with indecision about something we then ask God for inspiration and we let go of struggling for an answer. Alcoholics Anonymous says that you will be surprised at how the right answers will come after we have practiced this way of living. It also comes to pass that our hunches are more right than wrong. We also pause throughout the day when we are fearful, puzzled or anxious. We pray to the Higher Power for which direction to take. I like this suggestion the best when AA says that "we constantly remind ourselves we are no longer running the show, humbly saying to ourselves many times each day "Thy will be done." We are then in much less danger of excitement, fear, anger, worry, self-pity or foolish decisions. We become much more efficient. We do not tire so easily, for we are not burning up energy foolishly as we did when we were trying to arrange life to suit ourselves. By coming to the meetings and admitting our addictions we finally got in touch with these emotions that have all but shut down from an early time in our lives, when to feel, hurt too much. We now have the chance to let these feelings get displayed and expressed in the supportive and trusting environment of our newly chosen family of the Depressed Anonymous group. (12)

And again

At each DA meeting we hear different members of the group tell how the Higher Power helped return them to a peace, a serenity that they had never experienced until they started coming to Depressed Anonymous and began working on themselves. Now they can spend time in prayer and meditation with the Higher Power guiding their lives through the times of darkness. In time they have found giving up their depression to the care of the Higher Power almost a pleasure. It is our belief that if we want to begin to live, we must surrender our addiction to depression. The more we are tempted to seek comfort and bash ourselves with thoughts of how bad we are, the more depressed we become. But on the positive side the more we begin to take mastery over our thinking and listless behavior, the smaller, gradual gains we will make in seeing some light at the end of the tunnel. By living just for today, that is, one day at a time, and not in the hurts and pain of yesterday or the fear and anxiety of tomorrow, we will begin to see a spark of light coming over the horizon. (3)

..Meditation is likewise a waiting upon the Higher Power to reveal itself in our lives. We try daily to make conscious contact with the God of our lives as we understand God. We begin to love ourselves and each other, and when we attend our meetings we learn that it is in our openness to the Higher Power that this God of our understanding can operate. Our lives begin to assume a new hopefulness. (3)

Our program is a spiritual one. We are not a RELIGION WITH SET DOGMAS AND DOCTRINES but we are seekers of our true selves where we intend to find God and surrender our will to God. This small step can lead us to greater healing and hope. (3)

...Constructive meditation is the first requirement for each new step in our spiritual growth. (3)

On awakening, Let us think about the 24 hours ahead. We ask God to direct our thinking, especially asking that it be divorced from self-pity and from dishonest or self-seeking motives. Free of these, we can employ our mental faculties with assurance, for God gave us brains to use. Our thought-life will be on a higher plane when our thinking begins to be cleared of wrong motives. If we have to determine which of two courses to take, we ask God for inspiration, an intuitive thought, or a decision. Then we relax and take it easy, and we are often surprised how the right answers come after we have tried this for a while.

We usually conclude our meditation with a prayer that we are shown all through the day what our next step will be, asking especially for freedom from damaging self-will. (2)

In praying, our immediate temptation will be to ask for specific solutions to specific problems, and for the ability to help other people as we have already thought they should be helped. In that case, we are asking God to do it our way. Therefore we ought to consider each request carefully to see what its real merit is.

Even so, when making specific requests, it will be well to add to each one of them this qualification. (2)

Praying means to ask for something. We ask that we might let God take over our lives since we have admitted that we are powerless over sadding ourselves and that our lives have become unmanageable. As it says in Alcoholics Anonymous, "I saw that is was my LIFE that was unmanageable -

not just my drinking." I believe there is much wisdom in that short statement, and it is one that I want to reflect upon. The fact that we have pretty much shut ourselves off from the world is not a very sane thing to do when one of our human species major characteristics is being a social creature. (3)

In praying, we ask simply that throughout the day God place in us the best understanding of his will that we can have for that day, and that we be given the grace by which we may carry it out.

There is a direct linkage among self-examination, meditation and prayer. Taken separately, these practices can bring much relief and benefit. But when they are logically related and interwoven, the result is an unshakeable foundation in Life. (2)

Meditation is something which can always be further developed. It has no boundaries, of width or height or depth. Aided by instruction and example as we can find, it is essentially an individual adventure, something which each one of us works in his own way. But its object is always the same-to improve our conscious contact with God, with God's grace, wisdom and love. And let us always remember that meditation is in reality intensely practical. One of its first fruits is emotional balance. With it we can broaden and deepen the channel between ourselves and God as we understand God. (2)

Just sitting back and relaxing is a difficult thing to do when we are depressed, but if we want to have the Higher Power work in our lives then we have to quiet ourselves and listen often to its promptings. Listen then and pray. Pray that you might free this sadness in yourself as you continue to work the steps of these programs. The more you live with a gratitude attitude the more you will see that life is worth living and that you can live with the unpredictable. Life is supposed to be unpredictable and the reason why it is that each of us lets God's power unfold in our lives. ...It won't be long until our meditation will produce in us a feeling that God is guiding our lives and that its love is putting us back on our feet. We are finding that we want to risk testing out our wings and so we try to live one day at a time and forget about the hurts, fears and pain of yesterday, or the anxious moments that we might face tomorrow. The members of the group call these what if's – what if this happens or what if that happens, etc. The Higher Power is only today, it's not yesterday or tomorrow. It lives now. It lives in our hearts and all it wants and desires is that we make contact with it, and then its force will unfold as time continues. With time it will manifest itself, in our minds and hearts. (3)

I thank God every day for my freedom from my addiction, and I am now able to share my story of how God is working in my life with other members of the DA group. My healing, like yours, is now being passed along to all those persons whose depression has made their lives unmanageable. With our new found belief in a power greater than ourselves we are living manifestations of God's power at work.
Thy will be done! (3)

Sometimes it comes to our mind that we have prayed a long time and still it seems that we do not have what we ask for. But we should not be too depressed on this account, for I am sure, according to our Lord's meaning that either we are waiting for a better occasion, or more grace, or a better gift.

Julian of Norwich

Perhaps one of the greatest rewards of meditation and prayer is the sense of belonging that comes to us. We no longer live in a completely hostile world. We are no longer lost and frightened and purposeless. The moment we catch even a glimpse of God's will, the moment we begin to see truth, justice and love as the real and eternal things in life, we are no longer deeply disturbed by all the seeming evidence to the contrary that surrounds us in purely human affairs. We know that God lovingly watches over us. We know that when we turn to Him, all will be well with us, here and hereafter. (18)

I now end this manuscript with this wonderful prayer "God grant us the serenity to accept the things we cannot change, courage to change the things we can, and the wisdom to know the difference".

NOTES

References for Depressed Anonymous are listed with 2 numbers, the 1st number is referencing pages in edition 1 or 2 of the book and the 2nd number is referencing pages in edition 3 of the book (i.e. 36/39)

INTRODUCTION

1) Speaking of sadness	Page	194
1) Speaking of sadness	Page	195
2) As Bill Sees it	Page	1
3) Depressed Anonymous	Page	36/39

CHAPTER ONE

CHAPTER TWO

2) As Bill Sees it	Page	231
2) As Bill Sees it	Page	231
2) As Bill Sees it	Page	53
4) Alcoholics Anonymous	Page	10
4) Alcoholics Anonymous	Page	14
4) Alcoholics Anonymous	Page	13
4) Alcoholics Anonymous	Page	13
4) Alcoholics Anonymous	Page	13-14
4) Alcoholics Anonymous	Page	14-15
2) As Bill Sees it	Page	308
2) As Bill Sees it	Page	148
2) As Bill Sees it	Page	63
4) Alcoholics Anonymous	Page	494
2) As Bill Sees it	Page	87
2) As Bill Sees it	Page	1
3) Depressed Anonymous	Page	94/110

CHAPTER THREE

4) Alcoholics Anonymous	Page	507
5) Choosing, Not Losing	Page	340
6) Depression: The Way out of your prison	Pages	15-16
4) Alcoholics Anonymous	Page	43

CHAPTER FOUR

3) Depressed Anonymous	Page	109/127
3) Depressed Anonymous	Page	106/124
3) Depressed Anonymous	Page	109/127
3) Depressed Anonymous	Page	1
7) The Antidepressant Tablet	10/3, 4.	
18)	Page	75
3) Depressed Anonymous	Page	35/39
3) Depressed Anonymous	Page	4
4) Alcoholics Anonymous	Page	63
4) Alcoholics Anonymous	Page	100

CHAPTER FIVE

3) Depressed Anonymous	Page	105/122
8) The Infinite Way	Page	147
9) The Infinite Way	Page	146
3) Depressed Anonymous	Page	115/134
3) Depressed Anonymous	Page	107/125
3) Depressed Anonymous	Page	53/71
3) Depressed Anonymous	Page	141/159
3) Depressed Anonymous	Page	133/151

CHAPTER SIX

10) Believing is Seeing	Page	23
11) Mind as Healer	Page	303
3) Depressed Anonymous	Page	18/36
12) Depressed? Here is a way out	Pages	177-178

3) Depressed Anonymous	Page	129/147
3) Depressed Anonymous	Page	169/188
3) Depressed Anonymous	Page	58/76
3) Depressed Anonymous	Page	76/94
13) Wanting Everything	Pages	333ff

CHAPTER SEVEN

3) Depressed Anonymous	Page	167/185
3) Depressed Anonymous	Page	118/136
3) Depressed Anonymous	Page	118/136
3) Depressed Anonymous	Page	137/155
14) The Successful Self		
3) Depressed Anonymous	Page	78/96
16) The Antidepressant Tablet		
3) Depressed Anonymous	Page	95/113
3) Depressed Anonymous	Page	26/44
3) Depressed Anonymous	page	26/44
3) Depressed Anonymous	Page	89/107
3) Depressed Anonymous	Page	104/122
3) Depressed Anonymous	Page	122/140
3) Depressed Anonymous	Page	106/124
3) Depressed Anonymous	Page	128/146
3) Depressed Anonymous	Page	138/156
3) Depressed Anonymous	Page	143/161
3) Depressed Anonymous	Page	173/191
6) Depression: The Way out of your prison	Page	11
15) How to Find Hope	Page	1

CHAPTER EIGHT

3) Depressed Anonymous	Page	115/133
3) Depressed Anonymous	Page	26/44
3) Depressed Anonymous	Page	78/96
14) The Successful Self	Page	180/198
14) The Successful Self	Page	179/197

14) The Successful Self	Page	179/197
3) Depressed Anonymous	Page	21/39
3) Depressed Anonymous	Page	1/19
3) Depressed Anonymous	Page	57/75
3) Depressed Anonymous	Page	139/157
3) Depressed Anonymous	Page	153/171
3) Depressed Anonymous	Page	84/102
3) Depressed Anonymous	Page	45/63
3) Depressed Anonymous	Page	50/68

CHAPTER NINE

3) Alcoholics Anonymous	Page	187
16) The Anatomy of Melancholia	Page	170
4) Alcoholics Anonymous	Page	61
16) The Anatomy of Melancholia	Page	180
7) The Antidepressant Tablet		
4) Alcoholics Anonymous	Page	47
18) Twelve and Twelve	Pages	27-28
1) Speaking of Sadness	Page	102
3) Depressed Anonymous	Page	105/123
3) Depressed Anonymous	Page	179/197
18) Twelve and Twelve	Page	105
1) Speaking of Sadness	Page	193
4) Alcoholics Anonymous	Pages	46-47
2) As Bill Sees it	Page	171
17) International Conference on Depression	Page	134
17) International Conference on Depression	Page	135
3) Depressed Anonymous	Page	169/187
3) Depressed Anonymous	Page	169/187
18) Twelve and Twelve	Pages	124-125

CHAPTER TEN

2) As Bill Sees it	Page	127
3) Depressed Anonymous	Page	101/119
12) Depressed? Here is a way out	Pages	169-170
3) Depressed Anonymous	Page	27/45
3) Depressed Anonymous	Page	35/53
3) Depressed Anonymous	Page	36/54
3) Depressed Anonymous	Page	48/66
2) As Bill Sees it	Page	243
2) As Bill Sees it	Page	329
3) Depressed Anonymous	Page	94/112
2) As Bill Sees it	Page	33
2) As Bill Sees it	Page	150
3) Depressed Anonymous	Page	96/115
3) Depressed Anonymous	Page	109/127

REFERENCES

(1) Karp, David A (1996) Speaking of Sadness: Depression, Disconnection and the Meanings of Illness. Oxford University Press, NY.

(2) (1967) As Bill Sees it: The Way of Life –Selected writings of AA's co-founder. Alcoholics Anonymous World Services, Inc. NY.

(3) (1998, 2008) Depressed Anonymous. 2nd ed. Depressed Anonymous Publications. Louisville.

(4) Alcoholics Anonymous (1955), Alcoholics Anonymous World Services, Inc. New York City.

(5) Rowe, Dorothy (1978) Choosing Not losing. Wiley, Christopher and New York.

(6) Rowe, Dorothy (1983, 1996) Depression: The way out of your prison. 2nd edition Routledge, Kegan and Paul, London.

(7) The Antidepressant Tablet, Depressed Anonymous Publications, Louisville, KY 40217.

(8) Goldsmith, Joel (1979) The Infinite Way, DeVorss and Co., (31st Printing).

(10) Smith, Hugh (1999) Believing is Seeing. Depressed Anonymous Publications. Louisville, KY. 40217.

(11) Pelletier, Kenneth R. (1979) Mind as Healer, Mind as Slayer: A Holistic Approach to preventing Stress Disorders Delta. Philadelphia. Anonymous

(12) Smith, Hugh (1990) Depressed? Here is a way out. HarperCollins, Fount Imprint, London.

(13) Rowe, Dorothy (1994) Wanting everything.
Harper Collins Publishing, Ltd. London.

(14) Rowe, Dorothy (1993) The successful self.
HarperCollins Publications, Ltd. London.

(15) Smith, Hugh (1999) How to Hope.
Depressed Anonymous Publications, Louisville, KY.

(16) Burton, Richard (1948) The Anatomy of Melancholia.
Edited by E. Dell and Jorden-Smith (Tucker Publishing
Company, NY). (Originally published in 1621).

(17))Lorento, Aquilino Polaino. Is Depression Solely a matter
of medical intervention? From the proceedings of the XVIII
International Conference of Depression. Journal of the
Pontifical Council for Health/ Pastoral Care. Nov. 13-14-15,
2004, Rome.

(17b) Meggle, Dominique. Establishing Social Ties in a
society that is Broken Down and Devasated by
Individualism. In Dolentium Humani : Christ and Health in the
World. From the Proceedings of the XVIII International
Conference on Depression. Journal of the Pontifical Council
for Health/ Pastoral Care. Nov. 13-14-15, 2004, Rome.

(18) (1952, 1953, 1981) Twelve Steps and Twelve
Traditions. The A.A., Grapevine, Inc. and Alcoholics
Anonymous Publishing.

(19) Hugh Smith, (2000) The Promises of Depressed
Anonymous, Depressed Anonymous Publications,
Louisville, Ky.

www.ingramcontent.com/pod-product-compliance
Lightning Source LLC
LaVergne TN
LVHW051134080426
835510LV00018B/2415